ROSALINA'S STORY

A Trail of Mayhem

Rob Woutat

For Marilee

Also by Rob Woutat

Dakota Boy: A Childhood in Memory

Indelible Gifts:

The Story of a Twentieth Century American Family

CONTENTS

Where ever the criminal is – sauntering down the street, buying groceries at the supermarket, driving in rush hour traffic, riding the elevator to his apartment – he visualizes people and property as opportunities for conquest.

"Inside the Criminal Mind," Stanton Samenow

Author's Note

We're fascinated by people shockingly unlike us: Child molesters, rapists, murderers, the butchers of innocents, the architects of pogroms and ethnic cleansing and the foot soldiers who carry out the work, suicide bombers and other true believers who kill in the name of their gods - they're far more interesting than the rest of us. Who interests us more, Mother Teresa or Adolf Hitler? Miss America or the mother who kills her own children?

We're drawn to those who do things we can barely imagine anyone doing, who are indifferent to the harm they cause others, or even take pleasure in it, who are untroubled by their own viciousness, whose catalog of activities is aimed at satisfying their own needs at the expense of strangers and even their families.

This is a story about two such people. One of them, a woman, is certainly capable of telling her own story in her own words, in either of two languages. She would certainly prefer to, as she told it to me, but she would not tell it truthfully, a fact you'll recognize soon enough. She may not even be *capable* of telling it truthfully. As I learned through our conversations, she would leave out important things. She would subjugate truth to her imaginings. She would tell things that are patently not true while believing them to be true, all to fashion an ideal conception of herself and a world as she wishes it would be.

But to a lesser extent this is also the story of one of her husbands, an on-again, off-again lover, a man I haven't met because he declined to talk with me, a man I know only by his deeds, through newspaper accounts, through documents from the criminal justice system, and through people who knew him at various stages in his life.

I admit to some audacity in telling other peoples' stories, but it's important that the reader know the truth, so I'm telling her story, as truthfully as I can, believing that the truthful version is even more interesting than her own.

Most of this story took place in my county – Kitsap County on Washington's Olympic Peninsula – where it was easy enough to find the basic facts from old news clips at my local library, from investigators' reports by the sheriff's deputies, from people who knew the principal actors, and from interviews with the woman herself. Everything I know comes from those sources.

If you're a reader of murder mysteries, be warned that this story isn't one of them. Not exactly. While there is a murder here, maybe two or three, the identity of the killers becomes evident soon enough, so it's less a who-done-it that a how-done-it and a why-done-it.

It's also a portrait of two people and the mayhem they were destined to leave in their wake.

NOTE: An asterisk denotes a pseudonym.

ONE

A Body, December 22, 1981

On Tuesday morning December 22, 1981, 23-year old Yeoman 2nd Class William H. Edmondson didn't show up for work at the Bangor Submarine Base in Northwest Washington State.

The fact is noteworthy because Edmondson was a reliable worker. He joined the Navy after graduating from North Pocono High School in Scranton, Pennsylvania, in 1976, served four years, and left the Navy briefly before re-enlisting to serve another term. He had married only about four months earlier, which meant an additional $600 to his paycheck, so he and his bride had just bought a three-bedroom house in a pleasant middle-class community of split-level homes, split-rail fences, and tall Douglas firs, and to further celebrate his raise, his bride insisted on buying all new appliances.

Maybe he just overslept. Maybe he had a flat on his way to work, or was slowed by unusually heavy traffic, or a traffic accident. But later in the day when he still hadn't appeared or called his supervisor, the Navy police were notified, as were the police departments in the various communities in the county and the Kitsap County Sheriff's office.

Edmondson's Navy friend Mike Cogswell, who had shared an apartment with Edmondson and now lived with the newlyweds in an arrangement that allowed Edmondson to settle a debt, was especially worried. He began making phone calls, first to Edmondson's wife Rose at the hospital where she worked, but her shift hadn't started yet. He called the Washington State Patrol and AAA in case an accident had been reported. He called the hospital emergency room. He called some of Edmondson's other Navy friends, but nobody had any answers.

Days went by and he still didn't report for work or contact his supervisor, his wife, his mother in Pennsylvania — he always called her on Christmas — or any of the other people in his life.

Bill Edmondson liked to drink with his Navy friends and sometimes drank too much. When he drank too much, he talked too much and told stories his friend Cogswell and others found hard to believe, including a tale about having been born in prison after his mother was convicted for murdering his father. "He was kind of a bullshitter," Cogswell said. "You never knew whether to believe him or not."

Had he been drinking and gotten into a fight in a bar and been beaten up, maybe even killed, his body dumped in the woods? Kitsap County offers plenty of places to dump a body.

If you place your left hand on a table, with the fingers closed together but the thumb extended, you have a rough outline of the Olympic Peninsula in Washington's northwest corner, with the thumb representing the Kitsap Peninsula. It's on the opposite side of Puget Sound from Seattle. The peninsula would be an island but for a narrow isthmus at its southern end.

Although the county is one of the most densely populated in the state, its 566 square miles are heavily wooded, mostly with conifers, and the county is bounded by more than 250 miles of saltwater shoreline. If Edmondson had been killed, his body could easily have been slipped off a pier to be digested quickly by Dungeness crabs, or it could have been dragged deep into the woods where the killer wouldn't leave any tracks and where it might not be found for years except by animals, and then nothing would be left but a few scattered bones.

The morning of December 29, the temperature was below freezing but the sky was clear and intensely blue, a young man was out for a walk on one of the dirt roads that run through an 1800 acre Christmas tree farm in the southwest part of Kitsap County. Snow had dusted the young trees, and over their tops he could see the Olympic Mountains to the west, 40 miles away but seeming much closer with their fresh snow against a blue sky.

He came upon the body of a man face down in a puddle that had frozen over the night before. The body had light brown hair and was balding. His right arm was extended beyond his head; the left was under his body and extended toward his right. He was stripped to the waist despite the near-freezing temperature, and his white belt and blue jeans were pulled down to partially expose his buttocks. He wore powder-blue running shoes. At this elevation, the nighttime temperature had been below freezing so frost coated the body and the young conifers nearby. The puddle was frozen around his face.

When the detectives and crime scene specialists arrived from the Kitsap County Sheriff's office, they went about the slow, meticulous business of investigating the scene, measuring and photographing and sketching. They measured the length, width, and depth of the puddle and the size of a man's boot print near the body. They also measured the width of some tire tracks and the distance from the tire tracks to the body, and the distance from the body to the nearest entrance gate, noting that all entrances to the property were locked. They sketched the entire scene and photographed the body and the boot print and tire tracks and made casts of them.

They looked for anything and everything that might lead them in one direction or another – a tiny fragment of a candy wrapper, the plastic tip from a shoelace, a wad of saliva, a cigarette butt, a shell casing, whatever might give them a direction and maybe one day solve the case.

After hours at the scene, they broke the body free from the ice and turned it over. It was stiff from cold and the rigor of death. One investigator said it was like flipping a heavy sheet of plywood. They went through the young man's pockets and found a one-dollar bill, 56 cents in change, two keys on a key ring, and a military ID card in the name of Yeoman 2nd Class William Harold Edmondson. The photo on the card matched the victim.

Even without an autopsy report, the detectives could see enormous anger behind this death, and the partial undressing of the body and a man's boot print nearby suggested homosexual activity gone awry. The killer's failure to hide the body where it couldn't be found offered further suggestions: He was in a hurry, maybe a careless amateur, and he was vicious.

When the crime scene investigators finished their work, the body was driven to the medical examiner to be thawed out for processing.

On first glance, the medical examiner believed the victim must have been hit by a large truck traveling at high speed, but when he studied the body more closely, he saw four bullet holes in the head – two in the left temple and two more in the back. The left side of the body was badly bruised. By excavating the skull, he found bullets that came from a small caliber weapon fired at close range. The victim's eyes were swollen shut and his chest was caved in—there was a clear imprint of the heel of a cowboy boot in his sternum—and when the medical examiner opened the chest and abdominal cavities he found broken ribs, a heart perforated through the right ventricle, a ruptured spleen and a damaged liver.

The young man's blood alcohol content was .26, more than three times what qualifies in most states for drunkenness. To reach that level, a man his size would have had to drink the equivalent of several bottles of wine or eight martinis over a five-hour period. So at the time he died, it's likely he was in a stupor with impaired sensations, severe motor impairment, diminished understanding, and possibly even a loss of consciousness. Under these conditions, he was probably able to feel pain but likely oblivious to what was happening to him.

* * *

Bill Edmondson was the sixth child of Arthur and Janet Edmondson of Scranton, Pennsylvania. His father was too young to fight when the Americans joined World War II, but as soon as he qualified, he joined the Naval Air Force and served until war's end. When he came home to Scranton after the war he married 16-year-old Janet Efland, a junior at Central High School, and went to work as a truck driver for a company where her father was vice president and superintendent. The young couple also went to work having babies, the first born in 1947.

By the mid 1950s or maybe earlier, after the birth of their fifth child, the marriage began to crack because of frequent bickering about money and paying the bills. Arthur controlled the money but Janet bought the groceries and had to take out loans surreptitiously by forging her husband's signature. If she wanted 50 cents, she said in court documents, she had to ask him for it.

She claimed her husband abused her verbally and many times beat her with his fists, especially after he'd been drinking. On July 8, 1958, Janet Edmondson was six months pregnant with her sixth child. That night, after another round of fighting over money, Arthur threatened to either put her in jail or send her to a state hospital for acute psychiatric care. When they went to bed, he was angry and she was desperate. She tried to make up but he didn't want to bothered, told her he was going to leave and would come home only to sleep and to persecute her, then went to sleep.

Because of her pregnancy and the accompanying gain in weight, Janet had pain in her legs and back and had to get up several times in the night. On her way back to bed for the third time, she said later, "I was tight inside – my head and my stomach – I can't explain the feeling I had."

The Edmondsons kept guns in the bedroom, and Arthur had taught his wife how to shoot. "I went to the gun cabinet," she explained to the court, "and put a shell in the .32 caliber rifle. I walked over to the bed and stood there a couple of minutes. I didn't mean to kill him. I was only going to frighten him. I don't know *how* I was going to frighten him. I had no intention of killing him. I just know I pulled the trigger. I don't remember doing it. There was a big explosion in the room. I ran downstairs to call the police. I knew I had done something."

There was no trial because Janet Edmondson confessed her role in her husband's killing, but before he sentenced her, the judge heard testimony from a psychiatrist who interviewed Janet some months earlier, Janet Edmondson's aunt, Janet Edmondson herself, and the detectives who were called to the scene. The psychiatrist testified that Janet, by then about 30, was emotionally immature, insecure and unhappy because of the fights over money. He saw her as an "inadequate personality with tendencies to be impulsive in action." He believed that her current pregnancy opened up her feelings about her previous pregnancies. Her husband wouldn't talk with her about it and wouldn't go with her to her doctor appointments, the psychiatrist said. He added that the husband's behavior followed a pattern of rejection and indifference toward their children, who meant everything to Janet, and that that her mental condition at the time of the killing was aggravated by her pregnancy and her husband's hostility or indifference.

The aunt testified that Janet Edmondson had come to her home about two weeks before the killing and expressed her fears, but her husband, Arthur, arrived and took her home. The aunt later went to the Edmondson house where she found Janet hysterical. She also reported that she once asked Arthur why he'd didn't just leave his wife if he felt so hostile toward her, and that he replied, "I'm going to stay with her and torment her until she dies."

With the husband dead and the children so young, there was nobody to refute this testimony.

The judge decided that Mrs. Edmondson's crime constituted second-degree murder, which in Pennsylvania called for a maximum sentence of 20 years, but he called for a maximum of 10. After five years at the State Industrial School for Women, a program that focused on homemaking and basic education, she was paroled, and with the other five children farmed out to relatives, she was free to raise her sixth child, who was born in the Scranton State Hospital, one of the state's psychiatric institutions, while she awaited her sentencing. She named him William Harold Edmondson.

They moved to Moscow, 10 miles southeast of Scranton, where Bill – she called him "Billy " – grew up and went to school, graduating from North Pocono High School in 1958. He apparently made little impression on his classmates who, years later, had only vague memories of him: He was smart, he was quiet and stayed pretty much to himself, and he was good in math and science. They couldn't remember his taking part in sports or other school activities, and they didn't know if he ever dated.

Bill's classmates saw him as smart enough for college, but with little money available, he joined the Navy after high school, served for four years, left the Navy, then decided to rejoin. He was assigned to the submarine base at Bangor, Washington.

TWO

The Investigation Begins – December 29

After finishing at the crime scene and seeing to the transport of Bill Edmondson's body to the medical examiner, two detectives from the Kitsap County sheriff's office took charge of the case – Chief of Detectives Dave Morgan and Detective Ray Magerstaedt, both 32. Morgan wasn't a by-the-book, spit-and-polish company man. He didn't like paperwork and other government procedures, one colleague said, and should never have been appointed Chief; he was too indifferent to protocol. He was more the good old boy who made work fun by firing bottle rockets and having water fights in the office. "He liked to grab guys and wrestle with them," Magerstaedt said. "If you screwed up," another co-worker said, "he didn't berate you endlessly. He just said, 'Don't do it again.' Then you were OK with him." Morgan owned horses and lived at what he called "The Hard Scratch Ranch" about 10 miles north of Bremerton, the largest city in the county.

His partner, Magerstaedt, was slightly shorter, a few pounds lighter, a man who still played football, basketball and baseball. He had brownish-gray hair and a moustache and was in the early stage of balding. He was known as an intimidating interviewer who dug for answers, who was happy to leave the meticulous work of crime scene investigation to others so he could "go get the bad guys," as he put it. He had great respect for Morgan who, he said, was like a brother. "He was a stand-up guy, really respected. If Dave asked you to do something, you wanted to do it, just because it was Dave who asked. He was as good a detective as there ever was."

Magerstaedt wasn't as well liked as Morgan and wasn't as deft in working with others, so not many liked him, according to a colleague who described Magerstaedt as "an overall butt" and "an ass." "On the other hand," the colleague said, "you could *tell* him he was an overall butt and an ass."

By mid day, December 29, the two detectives learned that Edmondson's wife Rose worked in the kitchen at Harrison Hospital in Bremerton, the major medical center in the county. They drove to the hospital and invited her to come with them to the Sheriff's headquarters for a conversation. She did, without asking questions, following in her own car.

Beginning at 7:00 PM on the day Edmondson's body was found, detectives Morgan and Magerstaedt interviewed Rose at the sheriff's office after the reading of her rights. The brown-skinned woman who sat across the table from them was 27 and couldn't have been much over five feet tall. She was very slender and wore her black hair shoulder-length. She had wide-set almond-shaped eyes and full lips. She expressed no curiosity about having been called away from work, and she never mentioned that her husband had been missing for seven days.

With her accent and dark skin, she didn't appear to be American born, so Magerstaedt asked if she had any trouble understanding English? No, she said, she was fine.

She said the last she saw her husband was at The Sea Deck, a seafood restaurant in West Bremerton where they went to drink at about 6:00 or 6:30 the evening of December 21, but they began arguing when Edmondson saw her looking at a long-haired, bearded man nearby. Edmondson wanted the car keys so he could leave, but Rose told him he was too drunk to drive and withheld the keys from him. He left with the longhaired bearded man, she said. "To get some acid."

Quickly changing the subject, and with no apparent reason, Rose told the two detectives that her husband was gay, that she once walked in on him and his former roommate, Cogswell, and found them playing with each other naked in Cogswell's room. From that disclosure, shensaid that Edmondson was a liar and a drug user, that she'd paid for everything they had, and that she had no need for money herself. Accustomed to questioning everything at the beginning of an investigation, the detectives had to wonder if her allegations were true, or a false scent to send them off the trail.

On that same night, the night Edmondson disappeared, she got very drunk, she admitted, then left for another sailors' bar called Chugwater's where she drank some more and danced with sailors.

During this interview, when Magerstaedt finally broke the news to her that her husband was dead, that he'd been murdered, she started crying. "I was able to comfort her and talk with her," the detective said, "and she calmed down and said she'd continue answering my questions."

Rose had two cars, and Magerstaedt asked for her permission to search them both, the Monza and the Gremlin, but she was a little hesitant about the Gremlin, explaining that while it was her car, her friend Richard Manthie, who had just been released from prison in Montana, had her permission to use it. Reminded that she was the owner, and told that the detectives would ask Manthie before checking the car, she gave the permission they needed.

Magerstaedt continued the questioning, asking what happened after she left Chugwater's. She went to her friend Richard's house in Bremerton, she said, where they got into a fight, a verbal fight, she emphasized, adding that Manthie never hit her, although Magerstaedt noticed she had a black eye and a swollen nose. She explained that the injuries came when she hit her head on the steering wheel a few days earlier

Did she ever have a gun, Magerstaedt asked? Never, she said. She didn't know anything about guns, didn't even know how to hold one.

The detectives knew Mike Cogswell as Edmondson's friend and housemate who had called them to report Edmondson missing, so when

15

Magerstaedt told Rose he would talk with Cogswell about her allegations of homosexuality, she abruptly revised her story, said they weren't naked, they were in their underwear, and she wasn't sure if they were homosexuals. Sex with her husband was fine, she said. She loved him.

"What was he wearing when you left the house with him the evening of the 21st?" Magerstaedt asked. "A brown leather jacket," she answered, adding that he wore a wedding ring.

In his interview notes later, Magerstaedt wrote that at various times throughout the interview he told Rose he didn't believe many of the things she'd told him. For one thing, she quickly backed off the allegation of homosexuality. It appeared she didn't have her story straight yet. Still, a homosexual angle to the murder had to be checked out.

At no time, he noted, did she ask for a lawyer. And no, she said, she had never been to the tree farm where her husband's body was found, didn't even know where it was.

When she left Magerstaedt's office, she said, "I no kill my husband. I love my husband." But even after just this one interview, Magerstaedt knew that somehow she was directly involved.

THREE

Rosalina Misina Mendoza

October 1954—August 1977

There are at least two versions of the childhood of Rosalina Misina Mendoza. The first comes from a tattered certificate attesting to her birth in Manila, the Philippines, on October 3, 1954, to Mariano Mendoza, 33, a laborer, and Felicitas Misina, 36. The certificate of birth describes an infant with light olive skin and a mushroom shaped birthmark on her left thigh. Her birth parents, she told one of her future husbands, were killed in a jitney accident.

The second version, the one she told me years later, was that she was the illegitimate daughter of Ferdinand Marcos when he was a member of the Philippine House of Representatives, before becoming President of the Philippines. Her mother, Rose says, was one of his mistresses, a famous Filipino actress whose name Rose can't remember. (The mistress may have been Carmen Ortega, according to a Marcos biography, and Ortega was pregnant with his child when he met his future wife Imelda in early April of 1954. Marcos and Imelda married three weeks later.)

In Rose's version, the doctor warned the pregnant young actress that childbirth could kill her, but the mother-to-be declined an abortion and gave birth to Rose, dying in the process. "God must have really wanted me," Rose says.

17

Rosalina – sometimes called Lina, sometimes Rose – claims she was raised by her grandparents but that Marcos paid for her care, her expenses in a convent school, her living expenses afterwards, and later her airfare to the United States. She also told me she is closely connected to William Gates, Sr., father of the more famous Bill Gates, and that he owes her millions of dollars.

Her birth certificate includes a photo of her father, who is identified as a laborer and who looked nothing like Ferdinand Marcos. The future husband who says Rose's birthparents were killed in a jitney accident said Rose grew up on the streets of Manila and was placed in a convent school. As she tells her story, eventually she could no longer tolerate the nuns and the confines of the religious institution— "Nuns are kinda, ya know, strict," she explained—so while in the sixth grade she and a classmate waited until the nuns were asleep, then slipped out the door and escaped by bus 35 miles to Olongapo on the Bataan Peninsula, the location of America's Subic Bay Naval Station. Olongapo was the destination for undiscriminating young Filipino women and girls in search of American husbands. This is where 11-year-old Rosalina Misina Mendoza began meeting a long series of young American sailors and marines.

The naval station is closed now, but in the 1970s when Rose arrived and American ships were coming and going, the city was known for the bars that lined the edge of the base and served as a meeting ground for girls and lonely, randy young sailors.

The odor that overwhelmed the town arose from the sewage dump officially known as the

Olongapo River, and the predominant noise was that of bands blaring American rock music from the bars along the main street – Jimi Hendrix, Led Zeppelin, Grand Funk Railroad, Black Sabbath, and Deep Purple. Armed bouncers stood by the entrances, one hand within easy reach of a button that activated a light inside to alert contraband-carriers when local police were near. Inside, these places were muggy and poorly lit; some were air conditioned, others not; they differed mainly in the numbers of lizards and spiders on the walls.

Most of the bar girls said they came to Olongapo from distant villages to make money to support their families or to serve as substitute wives or girlfriends for lonely sailors. The bar girls had what one sailor called a "coconut telegraph system" that told them when American ships were arriving, so if you shipped off to Japan or Viet Nam you could count on your favorite girl to be waiting for you when you returned, if she hadn't already found someone to replace you and assure her passage to the U.S.

An American sailor who did a stint at Olongapo says the excessive friendliness of these girls set them outside the Filipino custom of decorum and formality. One sailor reported that when he went into the bars he was mobbed by 6-8 young girls pleading, "Buy me a drink," then, before he could respond, found one of them sitting in his lap. They were paid by the bar owner, and some of them, as young as 11, were making themselves available to men, especially American sailors who might some day be the widely coveted ticket to America.

Over the years American sailors fathered an estimated 52,000 children with these bar girls in different ports around the Philippines, about 3,000 in Olongapo. These Amerasian children were often orphaned, poor, and ostracized because of their mixed racial/ethnic makeup.

Even today, American sailors are using the Internet to find girls they knew in Olongapo in the 1970s:

"I am trying to locate a girl I knew from Subic City in 1987-1988. Her name is Linda Lamond. Please e-mail me with any info. Thank you."

"There was this girl at the "Cockeyed Cowboy" named Rowena, that I met in September 1986. She was very special to me. Anyone knowing of her whereabouts please contact me. Thank you."

"I'm looking for my old girlfriend from Subic Bay. Any one who can help me, I would be very greatful for your help. I have had it with the American women now and hoping I can find the one I should have never let go. For what ever its worth, I would be very greatful for any information that any one can give me. Her name she went by was Zingzing Rozelle. Not sure of the spelling so I'm sending a picture of her. If it helps, she use to work in a few of the clubs there just off the base. Thank you so very much guys."

"I served at the Cubi Point Marine Barracks between 1973 and 1975. I arrived there as an E-4 and left a E-5. During my time in the Philippines, I fathered a child by a Filipino lady named

ELIZABETH, she went by a nickname of LISA, which may have been spelled Liza. Have very little information to go on in my search, but hoped that maybe you could post my story on your site."

Despite the sordid reputation of these girls, one Navy veteran remembers that some of them were decent and said he knows of good marriages that came out of those meetings.

Many of those sailors met Rosalina, including 27-year-old corpsman Keith Ryan*. Through the Internet Ryan learned I was telling Rosalina's story, so he sent me emails about his relationship with her and later mailed a batch of letters she'd sent him. They started spending time together, he said, going to movies and playing golf, despite a great difference in their ages. She told him she was 15, although she says she was only 11.

"I first met Lina in Olongapo, P.I. in early 1971 at a bar called Old Jolo," Ryan wrote me. *"She was a hostess there and a very outgoing one at that. I was in the process of divorce and looking for someone to spend time with. I don't like bar hopping and I kind of liked Lina, so I stuck with her whenever I was in port. Everyone I knew that met her called her Crazy Lina. She would attack other women that tried to talk to me or anyone that tried to take advantage of her. She was always looking for ways to get money from me and I'm sure she had other sailors she worked when they were in port. ... I really didn't care what she did, I just wanted someone*

that I thought was safe and had a decent place to stay.

"My first cruise to the Philippines, I always stayed with Lina. The 2nd year I stayed on ship the first day in port. Some how she managed to get on base and on the ship. The Officer of the Deck called me on the intercom and made me get Lina off the base. From then on, I figured it would be easier to stay with her again than have her stalking me.

"The 3rd year when I went I returned to base, Lina was waiting at the gate with a baby. She said the baby was mine, but some of the girls she knew told me she had a Filipino boyfriend that got her pregnant. I didn't care as long as she was not mine. ... I thought about the timing and I was in Viet Nam when she got pregnant. She wrote me after I went back to the states and said she was pregnant again with my kid, but like the 1st kid, I wasn't there at the right time. I never saw her again."

How does Ryan explain the fact that the birth certificate of each child – one born October 5, 1972, the other on December 3, 1973 - lists Keith Ryan as the father? "In the Philippines you can get anything done if you're willing to pay for it," he said. Besides, she hoped that if she identified Ryan as the father, the two girls would become his legal and financial obligation.

Both birth certificates were prepared at the Office of the Local Civil Registrar and received in that office on August 25, 1984, almost 11 years after the birth of the second daughter, by which time Rose had been in this country for 11 years. Each child is listed as "Illegitimate." At least two other documents, one of them torn and tattered, purport to record the births, one listing Ryan as the father, the other naming another man.

Almost 30 years later and remarried, Ryan wrote me, "I really felt sorry for those little girls. Lina wrote us many times and we wrote her back. When she managed to get our phone number, she would call us collect. We stopped accepting her calls after a while, so she would call at 2, 3, 4 o'clock in the morning. She's hard to get away from, and she doesn't give up easily to get what she wants."

What Rose wanted above all was to get to America, a goal for many Filipinos for decades, a goal young men could reach by going to the Navy recruiting station in Olongapo and signing up. Once they served a few years as valets or cooks, they'd be on an expedited route to citizenship, and once they'd become citizens they could import their wives or fiancées, as Rose must have known.

For some Filipino women, a popular route was the one Rose was on, and as one Filipino immigrant told me, "Many of the women who come that way are prostitutes. Decent women don't take that route to the United States."

Another of Rosalina's prospects was a 20-year old Marine from Montana, Richard Wayne Manthie. Manthie and Rose planned to marry but he shipped out to other ports before they could arrange a ceremony.

Yet another, according to Rose, was an American sailor from Idaho whom she met at the N.C.O. club at Subic Bay. According to Rose's version, she became pregnant by him and gave birth to her second daughter in the Navy hospital, forgetting she'd claimed on their birth certificates that both girls were the children of Keith Ryan. It's possible she couldn't be certain who the father of either girl is.

This sailor didn't marry her either. Next she found the most promising ticket so far, another sailor, formerly a beverage truck driver from Chicago named James Thorpe* who agreed to file a fiancé visa petition on Rose's behalf on October 12, 1976, signifying his serious intent by listing his annual navy income ($5,796), his savings ($1,000), his personal property ($600), and the value of his Navy life insurance ($20,000). He provided this information, he wrote, "to prove I am responsible and capable of support of my fiancé, so to have her arrival in order for our marriage."

Her application for a visa indicates that she was 23 years old, with black hair (the photo shows it shoulder-length) and black eyes, that she had light brown complexion, that she was five feet, one inch tall, that her occupation was tailor, that the purpose of her trip to the United States was to marry her fiancé, who lived in Tacoma. In addition to the shoulder-length hair, the photo shows an oval face with wide set eyes and full lips. Knowing nothing more, it isn't surprising that young sailors would think her attractive, especially with her excessive friendliness and her eagerness to accommodate men.

That the handwriting on the application is not Rose's suggests that that she wasn't confident yet in English and that some one else filled it in.

Rosalina's fiancée visa was approved, and on April 17 of 1977, she entered the United States via Pan American Airlines, ready to become a bride. Her eleven-year effort to get to America had finally paid off.

She arrived at Washington's SeaTac airport without her two daughters. Quoting again a Filipino-American woman: "Bringing children over would have been a Filipino mother's first goal. Under immigration law, she could have brought them over, but she didn't."

When she got off the plane, Thorpe, her intended fiancé, was not there to greet her. She found him at his address in nearby Tacoma, but by then he'd either changed his mind about marrying her or was married already. Anyway, he called her a crazy prostitute, she says, and sent her away. Whether he ever really intended to marry her is unclear. It isn't unreasonable to wonder if they might have conspired to get her to America, if she might have given him money and sex in exchange for his submitting the required forms. Nor is it unreasonable to wonder if the immigration forms submitted in this sailor's name had actually been filled out by one of Rose's friends, with a forged signature. In puzzling over her immigration status two years after Rose arrived in the U.S., an American Vice Consul wrote on an INS form, "Was K-visa a ruse for her to enter US

In November 1977, Rose told a slightly different story of her arrival in the U.S. to an examiner from the Immigration and Naturalization Service, which was trying to sort out her status in this country. She said that when Thorpe didn't meet her at the airport some friends from Tacoma picked her up and she stayed with them in their apartment. After a few days she reached Thorpe and learned he was having second thoughts about marrying her.

Q. What happened when he came to the apartment?

A. We talk about – he said that, give me some more time. I want to think about it, I'm going to marry you or not. I said, "Why did you petition me if you are not going to marry me? Tell me right now, I want to know." And he just told me it's done. At the end of April. He always gets drunk then."

Rose told the examiner she tried to kill herself with pills but that her friends took her to a hospital to have her stomach pumped.

Years later when I first heard about Rose and curiosity drew me into her story, I discovered that this husband-not-to-be still lived in the Puget Sound area, but he didn't respond to my inquiries. If he'd been an accomplice to a fraudulent visa, it's understandable. He also may not have wanted to remember his having helped Rose get into this country because by then he undoubtedly knew the legal consequences. Or, if he was completely innocent of any immigration fraud, if Rose had submitted a fraudulent application without his knowledge, he may simply not want to remember that chapter of his life, or have a wife and family learn about it.

Whatever the case, Rose was now in a strange country on a visa requiring either that she marry within 90 days or be returned to the Philippines, so the pressure was on. She needed a husband urgently. She had gotten this far and was hardly willing to be turned back.

Rejected by her supposed husband-to-be, Rose was lugging her suitcase alongside Interstate 5 from Tacoma toward Seattle when a car stopped for her. The occupants were a Filipino couple from Bremerton, a blue-collar town of 27,000 across Puget Sound from Seattle, and recognizing her as another Filipino, a young woman apparently in a predicament, they stopped to talk with her. She told these good Samaritans about her arrival in SeaTac airport and about having just been rejected by her fiancé. This sympathetic couple drove her to Bremerton where she was welcomed by an extensive Filipino community.

* * *

In 1891 the U.S. Navy recognized Sinclair Inlet on Puget Sound as a promising deepwater port with strategic significance, so it bought 190 acres of shoreline property from German immigrant William Bremer for $9,512, and founded the Puget Sound Naval Shipyard, which soon became the largest employer on the Kitsap Peninsula. Ever since,

Bremerton has had a risky, unhealthy dependence on the Navy for its economic wellbeing.

In its earliest days, Bremerton was such a bawdy town, that in 1901 the Secretary of the Navy ordered an embargo of the new shipyard until the town cleaned itself up. His complaint was that sailors were routinely drugged and robbed between the time they left the shipyard exit and arrived at the steamer dock just a few hundred yards away. (Subsequent events in this narrative will suggest that during Rose's tenure in town, things hadn't changed much.) The mayor denied the city harbored opium dens and numerous "houses of ill fame operated by disreputable women. There are but two recognized prostitutes in the city. They live in shacks on the bay front."

The city placated the Navy and the Navy returned, and with the Shipyard on its way to becoming the second largest industrial employer in Washington after The Boeing Company, Bremer's lots sold fast. Bremer died a rich man, and the city named for him, platted in 1891, became the largest in the county.

By the time Rose arrived in Bremerton, the population of the county had grown seven times faster than the rest of the state's and had reached 147,000. The shipyard, the nearby facility where torpedoes are tested, and the new submarine base at Bangor employed more than a third of the county's population. The thousands of sailors meant happy hunting for the prostitute from Olongapo, but Bremerton was stagnant.

With the Navy presence, Bremerton has a transient population and a disproportionate number of rental houses, many of them run-down; its citizens weren't always quick to pass school levies, seeing education not so much an end in itself but as training for jobs. Ferry riders from Seattle who landed at the ferry dock, a one-block distance from a Shipyard entrance, saw tattoo shops (there are 11 in the county), dingy bars and vacant stores.

It was unexpected good luck for Rose that she'd arrived in a city with not just a large number of sailors – a group of people with whom she was intimately familiar – but a large Filipino community. Over the decades, Filipino men who'd served in the American Navy found work in the Puget Sound Naval Shipyard and enjoyed a quick path to American citizenship. They imported their wives and fiancés, and in time there were enough of them to have their own newspaper—the *Kitsap Filipino News*. They formed seven or eight groups like the Filipino American Community and the Northwest Ilocandia Association, organizations that served as large surrogate families for new arrivals and helped perpetuate their culture.

But Rose's primary need wasn't blending in with the Filipino culture. It was finding a husband.

The couple that rescued Rose along Interstate 5 and brought her to Bremerton introduced her to another Filipino couple, Vincent and Marietta Barrios. Vincent Barrios was well connected and influential in the Filipino community and, like everyone else Rose met, being immigrants themselves, he and his wife sympathized with her and her predicament. Through his work at the shipyard, Barrios had a friend named Agapito "Pete" Dugeno, a 76-year-old Filipino widower who'd retired from the shipyard and owned a small one-bedroom house where he lived alone on three and a half acres at the end of a dirt driveway off Anderson Hill Road in rural Port Orchard, South Kitsap County. A neighborly, gregarious man who'd throw a party on short notice, he was well liked by all his neighbors, including children, whom he liked to do things for and who were impressed that he'd been a minor league baseball player. He was a small, wiry man, about five feet four, just slightly taller than Rose. He'd had tuberculosis but now was healthy and fit.

Rose was charismatic, Marietta Barios said; she was persuasive and resourceful and knew how to approach people, especially men—a skill perfected through her work on the streets of Olongapo.

Dugeno was lonely but not desperate. As much as he wanted to be married again, he wasn't willing to wed the first prospect that came along. He'd turned down a 30-year-old woman for not being pretty enough, but when Marietta Barrios introduced him to Rose, he realized his expectations had been met. On June third, 1977, about two weeks after he and Rose were introduced (and a safe 43 days before her INS-imposed deadline) they were married by a

30

Baptist minister at the Kitsap County Court House in Port Orchard, the ceremony followed by a reception at the Legion Hall for Dugeno's friends and neighbors.

Was Pete Dugeno merely doing Rose a favor to solve her immigration problem, or was he genuinely happy to share the tail end of his life with an attractive young wife more than half a century younger than he? Both possibilities could be true. Some claimed he was embarrassed to have a wife so much younger; others said he was glowing at the reception, proud to have such a young bride.

Her marriage would get the Immigration and Naturalization Service off her back so she could settle comfortably into a new, secure American life and leave the prostitute's life behind. Or so she may have thought.

INS records note that Dugeno was born in 1900 and Rose in 1954. "Question as to whether this is a bona [sic] marriage, an INS investigator wrote." Her status in this country was a puzzle for the immigration officials. In an INS interview, Rose was asked how many times she dated Dugeno before they were married. She was accompanied in the interview by an attorney who objected to the question. The examiner said that if she refused to answer, he'd draw his own conclusions, and the interview continued.

"How many times did you date your husband before you married?"

"Many times."

"Did you date him in Bremerton, or other places?"

"No, he came down at my friend's house and picked me up and brought me up to his house. Since that, he told me to live there in the house. And then I moved with him, and he say, 'In the first week of June, I'm going to marry you.' I told him, 'Are you sure you're going to marry me? I just go back to the Philippines.' He said, 'No, you are not going back to the Philippines. I want to marry you.' He married me there."

Although she would later testify falsely to the INS examiner that she and Dugeno lived together as husband and wife for four months, only a month after the wedding, in late June of 1977, Dugeno confided something alarming to a neighbor in a conversation at the mailbox. He wanted to get a divorce, he told the neighbor, adding, "She's going to kill me." And on July, 2, 29 days after the wedding and 18 days before Rose was originally to be returned to the Philippines under her original fiancé visa deadline, she called the authorities in the night to report that Dugeno died in his bed at about 3:00 AM. His was the first body in Rosalina's wake.

The coroner at the time, a brother-in-law of a local funeral director, was in law enforcement but retired on disability before being elected coroner, and he wasn't trained in death investigation. He operated out of his house, and he had emphysema so he didn't go out on calls himself but sent his assistants, who weren't well trained either. Finding an old man dead in his bed at 3:00 AM, they just assumed the cause of death to be a coronary occlusion, as they wrote in their report, and saw no reason for an autopsy or inquest. But a coronary occlusion can be identified as a cause of death only through an autopsy, and with no autopsy performed, the examiners were merely guessing. A better-trained, more thorough medical examiner would have lifted Dugeno's eyelids to look for petechiae, the broken blood vessels that are an almost-certain sign of strangulation.

Records showed that Dugeno had named Rose as his sole beneficiary. She would inherit his house, which was paid for, and a small bank account.

Immediately after Dugeno's sudden death, one neighborhood couple took Rose into their home to comfort her. She cried a lot at first, but to show her gratitude she gave them some Filipino embroidery work, showed them how to prepare lumpia, pancit and squid, and taught them a few words of Tagalog. "She was sweet and likable," the wife said. "I could see how a lonely old man would take a liking to her."

But most neighbors' sympathies were with Dugeno, not with his young bride. One neighbor said mysteriously, " His death was not an accident. Valium is a powerful drug," but she gave no further explanation, and she wanted her name withheld. "For my own safety," she added. The neighborhood gossip was that she'd smothered him with a pillow, a rumor difficult for many to believe, given his physical fitness and Rose's diminutive size.

"The longer I knew her," another neighbor said much later in hindsight, "the more I felt that in a hug she might slip a knife in my ribs. She never made me feel I was being used exactly, but I did feel she was dishonest. Nothing I could put my finger on – just a feeling."

As it happens, military records show that Richard Wayne Manthie, the Marine who hoped to marry Rose when he was stationed at Olongapo, was at this time stationed at the 29 Palms Marine Base in California but was on leave to Kitsap County about the time of Dugeno's death. And there is this from a reporter who covered the story of Edmondson's murder: "Rose is a master manipulator, and Manthie was so smitten he'd do anything for her."

FOUR

Richard Wayne Manthie

1957—1977

Richard Manthie, born in the Bitterroot Valley of Western Montana in 1957, grew up in Superior, pop. 88, the fifth of nine children. Despite its natural beauty and the opportunities for outdoor recreation – fishing, hunting and hiking among the forested slopes of the Bitterroot Mountains—the Bitterroot Valley is a tough place to earn a living.

His father worked a bulldozer in construction and logging and was injured once when his bulldozer rolled over on him. Sometimes he had to go as far as Alaska to find work, leaving his wife with the nine children. "He was a smart guy, ingenious, hard working, always a hard worker," one neighbor said. "I thought the world of him."

But neighbors didn't speak as highly of the rest of the family. "[The mother] wasn't much of a housekeeper, and she took no pride in her appearance," said one. "She rode the school bus 12 miles to get groceries, and in cold weather she wore a diaper over her head for warmth. Her legs were so dirty, you couldn't tell where her dress stopped and her legs began."

At one time the family lived in an area locally known as "Dirty Corner," near a large, unsanctioned dump full of old cars, old machinery, decaying lumber and rotting telephone poles. "A mountain of debris," one neighbor called it. "Their house was small – about 16 by 40 – a log house with a scabbed on lean-to. It was so dirty, you didn't want to go in there."

It's hard to find water around there—one land owner had to drill three times before he found any— so the Manthies had a gravity-fed water supply with a tap in the kitchen sink. They had electricity but had to heat water on the stove for bathing. "They may have had an outhouse, a neighbor said. "The house never looked like it was finished. It must have been freezing cold in winter. It's torn down now."

That same neighbor said the parents would go into town to the bars at night, especially Friday nights, sometimes until 2:00 AM. "They'd bring the youngest kids with them and leave them in the old Ford station wagon while they were in there drinking, and the car stank of dirty diapers."

"I'm sure there was drinking and violence in the family," another neighbor said. "The kids had a rough life." Another amplified: "The boys always looked dirty and were made fun of because of the clothes they wore. They were a rag tag bunch, scrappers, in trouble a lot. If there was a ruckus on the playground, they were probably in it. They were often in trouble in school. They seemed to be trouble-bound."

One local couple who held vacation Bible school classes and church services in their home caught one of the Manthie boys stealing church money from the house and said he also stole a teacher's purse at school. A contemporary of the Manthie children said his parents wouldn't allow him to play with them.

Many of the Manthie children were discipline problems, neighbors said, even though the parents were completely intolerant of misbehavior. Later in his life, Richard described punishments delivered with fists and beatings with electric al cords, allegations that a psychologist believed to be credible.

Richard, like some of his siblings, had problems in school from the beginning and, because of social problems and learning difficulties, had to repeat three grades. Others considered him stupid. Even his brothers and his mother made fun of him because of his poor school performance. He completed the ninth grade but was expelled during the tenth grade for truancy.

His first recorded conflict with the law began at about age 10 when he was placed in juvenile detention for "joyriding" as official records put it. When he was 13, he began running away and was returned to detention at his mother's request, then was placed in multiple foster homes. At 14 he was arrested for trespassing and went back to detention for two weeks, and at 15 and 16 he was in two foster homes and one group home, all unsuccessfully. At 16 he was involved in the theft of some tires. By that time no foster home would take him and he was committed to a juvenile institution.

When he was released 17 he did something unusual for a boy so resistant to external discipline: he enlisted in the Marines, partly because he couldn't get a job, partly because he wanted to travel, he said, and partly because he hoped the Marines would give him an education. He enjoyed the military life at first, he said much later, but he quickly came to dislike it, "because of all the bullshit." He complained that new recruits had negative attitudes toward their military commitment.

He denied having any disciplinary problems while in the service, also denying having spent 30 days in the brig for one incident, but later reports indicated that he'd admitted having some trouble performing his military duties and getting along with blacks in his unit.

During part of his four-year tour with the Marines, he was stationed for about three months at the Subic Bay Naval Station in the Philippines, and this is where he met Rosalina Misina Mendoza. They planned to marry, but Manthie's ship left Subic Bay before they could arrange the ceremony. The final stop in his military career was at Twenty-nine Palms Marine Base in Southern California, where he arrived in June 1977. His life was soon to overlap again with that of Rosalina Misina Mendoza, now the young widow Rosalina Dugeno.

FIVE

Rosalina Dugeno and Richard Manthie

1977 – 1981

Rose and Richard Manthie remained in contact during his military tour, and when he returned to Montana for a visit in June 1977, shortly after her marriage to Dugeno, Rose drove there from Kitsap County to meet him. Records show that around the time of Dugeno's death on July 2, Manthie was on leave to Kitsap County. Did Rose solicit his help by assuring she'd become the beneficiary of Dugeno's meager estate? Rose says no, that Manthie was not in Kitsap at the time. With no autopsy, and because authorities knew nothing yet of Richard Manthie, or of his relationship with Rose, or that Manthie might have been in Kitsap when Dugeno died, there was nothing suspicious about Dugeno's death.

When Manthie returned that summer for duty to his Marine base at Twenty-nine Palms, Rose went with him, and on August 13, about six weeks after Dugeno's death, they were married at the Wee Kirk O' the Heather, one of the many quickie wedding services in Las Vegas. They began fighting soon after the ceremony but paused long enough for Rose to bear a child, a girl they named Valery*, born in Twenty-nine Palms on May 29, 1978. The identity of the girl's father is unclear. The birth certificate, dated six days after the child was born, lists Manthie as the father, but in a letter to me years later he said he adopted her. Assuming a nine-month gestation,

Dugeno is out of the picture; he died 10 months before the girl was born. Later in this narrative, Rose will give her own answer to the question.

Rose's newest husband was of medium height and weighed about 225 pounds. He had light brown hair, a square, chiseled face and a stocky build. Some, mostly men, described him as ordinary looking; others, mostly women, say he was movie-star-handsome. Some said he had average intelligence while others thought him slow and easily led. Most agreed, though, that he was pleasant when sober but resistant to authority and explosively violent when drunk, and he liked to drink.

The newlyweds lived at Twenty-nine Palms until Manthie's honorable discharge from the Marines in September 1978, and during his last year with the Marines he made several trips to Montana's Bitterroot Valley where he was incapable of staying out of trouble. He was charged with speeding and fined $100. After his military discharge, the couple lived for a short time in Florence, Montana.

The newlyweds separated for a few months after the wedding and Rose returned to Kitsap County where she found work at the NCO club at the Bangor sub base. She was fired from that job but found work in the kitchen at Harrison Hospital in Bremerton, a sandstone colored building on a hillside with a view of much of the city and, on a good day, the Olympic Mountains. At the hospital she met another employee, Robert Clovis Erickson, 57, a friend of her late husband "Pete" Dugeno. The two men had worked together at the shipyard. Erickson was a welder until poor health forced him out of the job and he found work in the security department of the hospital.

Erickson, a widower, lived alone in a small, two-bedroom, one and a half story house surrounded by trees on Long Lake Road in Port Orchard across Sinclair Inlet from Bremerton in a part of the county that might be categorized as semi-rural disheveled. To get to the house, you turned off Long Lake Road onto a one-lane dirt road that crossed a short wooden bridge over a creek. From there you curved to the right and in about 75 yards you came to a small house surrounded by hardwoods. The house itself had small windows and was covered with faux brick siding.

Erickson was tall and slender, about six feet, with glasses, gray hair and a ruddy face. His supervisor at the hospital described him as "a nice, laid back, mild- spoken guy, squared away. Everybody liked him. But he wasn't overly joyous. He was lonely, so he was always willing to work extra shifts because he had nothing else to do."

With emphysema and heart problems, Erickson had to cut back his hours at the hospital and eventually quit work altogether, so the apparently compassionate Rose became a housekeeper and companion for him, doing his laundry and other household chores.

In early 1979, Manthie rejoined Rose in Bremerton and the two of them rented a small house on Pennsylvania Avenue. Manthie found work as a janitor at the Washington Athletic Club in Seattle, commuting an hour each way by ferry across Puget Sound, and soon after that, at a Dyno Battery business in Bremerton.

But Western Montana kept pulling him back, despite the eight and a half hour drive on I-90 over the Cascade Mountains, across the expansive wheat fields of Eastern Washington, and through the forests of Northern Idaho, and despite all his previous problems there with his family, with school and the law. He was there again in April 1979, when a patrolman saw him driving recklessly and began a pursuit. Another patrolman set up a roadblock but Manthie drove around it, and both officers continued the pursuit, finally stopping him in Florence. Manthie was arrested but tried to get back into his car, and when a patrolman tried to stop him, Manthie threw him to the ground. The second patrolman finally handcuffed Manthie and forced him into a sitting position near one of the patrol cars, but Manthie got up and began banging his cuffed hands against the patrol car and broke the windshield.

He was charged with destroying state government property and disturbing the peace. Because the damage to the vehicle exceeded $150, his act was a felony. Oddly, the District Court record says nothing about speeding, eluding the patrolmen, or assaulting one of them to resist arrest. In September 1979, he pled guilty to criminal mischief and admitted he had no legal cause to show why the court's judgment should not be imposed. A judge deferred the sentence for three years on condition that Manthie stop drinking, get alcohol counseling, report to a parole officer, and pay the court $717.84 for damage to the patrol car. Those who knew Manthie, and Manthie himself, must have known that all this was simply too much for him to obey. As his Marine record showed, he wasn't especially amenable to rules that inconvenienced him.

Inexplicably, what the judge didn't know was that three months before he deferred Manthie's sentence, a court in nearby Missoula County had issued a warrant for Manthie's arrest on charges of rape and burglary, alleging that after meeting a young woman in a bar in Missoula, he went with her to her home in the Blue Mountain Trailer Court where he raped her and stole her billfold.

Manthie gave Rose this version of events: He and a friend went to a tavern where they were drinking beer and shooting pool when two prostitutes picked them up. "Rick is a hot tamale," Rose interjected. "He likes his sex." She described him as good looking, macho, with a "nice body," adding that he was so handsome that her Filipino friends all wanted to borrow him for a night. So as Manthie told it to Rose, the two men followed the girls to the trailer court where "both got blow jobs." As Manthie was about to leave, "his" girl, then 17, asked for money. He claimed to be surprised. "I thought we were just going to have a good time," Rose quoted him as saying. Manthie left without paying and soon took a bus back to Bremerton.

When Rose got home from work, she found that he'd cleaned the house, cooked dinner, and placed a lighted candle on the table. "We had a good time that night," she said with a wink.

The next day, the Kitsap County sheriff came to the house and arrested him for rape and burglary, the warrant alleging that besides the rape, he'd stolen money from the girl's trailer. "It's a long story, honey," he told Rose before he was taken to the Kitsap jail to await extradition to Montana. Rose seemed to be proud to be able to say that it was the governor himself who issued the extradition order.

Rose visited him frequently in the Kitsap jail to bring him money and clothes until his extradition to Montana where he pled not guilty on the rape and burglary charges and was released on $10,000 bail.

While Manthie was occupied with his legal problems in Montana, Rose was cultivating Erickson, the friend of the late Pete Dugeno. His wife Myrtle May had died, leaving him three stepchildren, but on January 30, 1980, soon after Rose befriended him, he signed a new will that expressly excluded his three stepchildren and left his entire estate to "my friend Rosalina M. Manthie." He also stipulated that should Rose die before him, his estate should pass not to his three stepchildren but to Rose's three daughters – the one Manthie adopted – Valerie - and the two she left behind in the Philippines. Like Dugeno, he also named Rose as his executrix.

On March 6, about five weeks after making out his new will, Erickson died and became Body Number Two in Rosalina's wake. Official documents showed heart failure as the cause of death, as they did in Dugeno's case. Given Erickson's poor health, there was no call for an inquest, and six days later Rose took over his house. Her former neighbors on long Lake Road and others who'd come to be suspicious of her were convinced she'd somehow contributed to his death. One said enigmatically, "She wrapped him around the bedpost." Others believed she'd encouraged him to drink and smoke, contrary to his doctor's orders.

As sole beneficiary of Erickson's estate, Rose inherited the house at 2299 Long Lake Road, which was a little bigger than the one she inherited from Dugeno. Like her earlier house, it was set back from the road and surrounded by trees, so it was not easily visible to neighbors, but it had two bedrooms and a storage room, and it had a second floor.

The court valued the house at $50,000; Erickson also had more than $23,000 in stocks and bonds and $500 in cash; personal property valued at $2,000; and a 16 year old Buick, a 16 year old Chevrolet pickup truck, and a 24 year old VW Karman Ghia—all three vehicles valued at no more than $1,000. The total estate came to $75, 686.50. Things were looking up for the poor little immigrant from the Philippines.

Among those suspicious of Rose's assistance to Erickson as he neared the end of his life were his three stepchildren, all prospective heirs. Believing Rose had wormed her way into Erickson's mind and turned him against them, they brought suit in the Kitsap County Superior Court in an attempt to block Rose's inheritance of Erickson's estate. They had already removed furniture from the house, and now they requested a temporary restraining order against Rose, believing she'd conceal or sell estate property before the will was adjudicated. In addition, they requested the appointment of a second administrator of the estate to guard the estate assets from Rose.

Another suit was brought by Edyth Clovis, a woman who had done housework and shopped for groceries for Erickson before Rose elbowed her out of the picture. Clovis sought $16,362.12, claiming that Erickson had not repaid loans or paid her for her work.

After examining the securities in Erickson's estate, Rose's lawyer requested the sale of $10,783 worth of stock that he saw as inappropriate for an unsophisticated investor but recommended she hold on to 100 shares of IBM and 200 shares each of Westinghouse and Public Service Company of Colorado, now Excel Energy.

Recognizing that further legal action would merely diminish the proceeds of the Erickson estate, Rose and Erickson's three stepchildren settled in August, with Rose agreeing to pay the plaintiffs

$15,000 and allow them to keep the personal property already in their possession. But as she did with Dugeno's estate, she began seeing her newest inheritance nibbled away by attorney's fees and estate taxes. Lunch wasn't as free as she might have thought.

In mid 1980, while Rose was preoccupied with preserving as much as she could of Erickson's estate, Manthie was continuing to have troubles of his own. In May, he'd been charged in Kitsap County again with speeding; in mid July he and Rose separated, with her living on Long Lake Road in Port Orchard and him in the small house they'd rented in Bremerton. Four days later he was charged again with speeding. In August, they reunited, but Manthie was charged with assaulting her and she filed for divorce, requesting separate maintenance. She alleged he'd abandoned her without cause and without funds, even though he was earning about $1,600 a month. She claimed that he stole things from her house, that he beat her severely enough to cause a concussion, and that he threatened to take their daughter out of the state. She asked for a restraining order and $400 per month in support, which the court granted. But the judge was reluctant to grant a divorce and persuaded them to wait 90 days before going forward.

In August 1980, with Manthie living in Bremerton and Rose in Port Orchard, she went to McGill's Tavern in Bremerton where she met another sailor, Mark Johnson, a yeoman 1st class stationed at the shipyard in Bremerton. When Johnson mentioned he was looking for a place to stay, Rose suggested he move in with her at her house on Long Lake Road, a house he later described as "quite spacious and beautiful," even though the roof leaked and most people called it a dump.

Johnson claimed that he and Rose developed a close but platonic relationship. He believed Rose to be divorced and knew she owned another house besides the one on Long Lake Road. After he moved in with her, Rose tried to persuade him to make her daughter Valery the beneficiary of his Navy life insurance policy. He may never know how wise he was to decline.

* * *

In October 1980, Manthie was back in Montana for his trial in Missoula County District Court on the charges of burglary and rape. The state had 22 witnesses to support its charge, including two doctors from the Missoula Community Hospital, two crime lab technicians, six people from the sheriff's office, and the alleged rape victim herself. On October 3, after a five day trial, the jury couldn't agree on the rape charge, thus sparing Manthie a two-to-20 year sentence, but it did find him guilty of burglary, which had a maximum penalty of 10 years' imprisonment. He was released on the $10,000 bond posted earlier.

But three days after the burglary conviction in Missoula County, Richard Manthie's repeated arrests for speeding, assault, drinking, and failing to report to his parole office finally brought him to the end of his rope. The judge, who had deferred sentencing after Manthie's earlier encounters with Montana's police officers, revoked probation and sentenced him to five years in the state prison at Deer Lodge. Inexplicably, at the close of the court session the judge categorized Manthie as a non-violent offender. In time, he would have reason to wish he had found otherwise.

* * *

In February 1981, with Manthie in prison and thus Western Montana a lot safer, Rose, now divorced, met another in a long series of sailors: 23-year-old Yeoman 2nd class William Harold Edmondson of Scranton, Pennsylvania.

They met at the enlisted men's club at the Bangor sub base where she still had privileges through her marriage to Manthie and where she met many other men. "We used to go there a lot to drink," recalled Mike Cogswell, Edmondson's Navy friend. "Bill was friendly. Got along with everybody. But he bragged a lot about his past Navy experiences and accomplishments, things a guy with his limited Navy experience couldn't have done. He lied so much, you never knew whether to believe him or not.

"We talked a lot about women. Like guys do. He was lonely, and I think he was looking for love. Probably Rose gave him attention, and that attracted him. Maybe as a single child he didn't get enough love. He never talked about marriage, but in the Navy you're better off if you're married. You got $600 more a month."

With Mark Johnson staying in Rose's house on Long Lake Road, Rose moved in with Bill in an apartment near Bremerton's Rolling Hills Golf Course, an apartment he shared with his friend Cogswell.

In early August 1981, with his Navy tour up, Mark Johnson prepared to return to his home in Albuquerque. By then, he told me by phone, he knew there had been many men in Rose's life, and he and many of the people he met through Rose often wondered how she was able to live in the style she did on her minimum wage job at the hospital. He questioned how she had several vehicles and always seemed to have plenty of money for personal possessions and entertainment. He answered his own question when he acknowledged that on the night before his flight to New Mexico, he, Rose and Valery stayed in a motel and that during the night Rose stole $400 from him. She paid back only $60.

During the time he lived with her on Long Lake Road, Johnson said, she had a number of lovers, both civilians and navy servicemen. "She usually ended up taking them for all they were worth," he said. "The relationships often ended in fights." He remembered being told that on two occasions Rose pulled a knife and a gun on her lovers, and he said that on a trip to Vancouver, Washington, she pulled a knife on him.

* * *

During that summer and fall of 1981, Edmondson kept a small, green, three by six-inch notebook in which he recorded memos and observations. On an undated page, apparently written while he, Rose and Cogswell were still living in their shared Kariotis apartment, he wrote,

Lost/Taken List

1. Gold watch, bought @ Allen's jewelry

2. Her gold watch also bought @ Allen's jewelry

3. Sanyo AM/FM cassette, B+W TV portable. Stolen from van same night Rose visited me at apartment (2600 NE Athens Way – Apt. C-6, Kariotis Apts)

4. $400 from room @ Holiday Inn. Rose + myself only ones in room. Door locked

5. Gold necklace w/3 horse heads on gold medallion.

6. 24 asst. tapes

7. Electric Guitar

Recommend check Hock-Shops

Sometime before mid August, before they wed, Rose convinced Edmondson that she was pregnant with his baby (she wasn't) and they married August 21, 1981, at the courthouse in Seattle. The next day they left on a honeymoon, driving eastward toward Montana and stopping in Deer Lodge, the location of the state prison, where they stayed in a motel. When Edmondson awoke the next morning, Rose was gone, and he noted his suspicion in his journal that she'd disappeared to visit Manthie.

On the night of August 28, just after the honeymoon trip to Montana, a strange incident occurred at the Kariotis apartment the newlyweds still shared with Cogswell. Cogswell returned to the apartment and found it in shambles. Two people had been fighting, reports said. Edmondson went berserk and raced around the apartment nude and threw things out the windows. Police arrived and took him to the Navy hospital.

Later, when asked what happened that night, Edmondson said, "I don't know, an overdose of Tylenol, or something like that." Later he told his Navy supervisor that Rose drugged him or put something in his drink and tried to poison him. At the hospital, under hypnosis, he told a psychiatrist that the last thing he remembered was Rose sitting on his chest and cramming Tylenol down his throat. Edmondson was allergic to Tylenol. It was the first attempt on his life.

On an undated page in his journal, Edmondson wrote, *Psychiatrist – NRMC   Bremerton*

Dr. Barley. Believe drugged + and given substance.
Referred to Inspector Cordell of PAN-AM Security
also is handling case. ... Extremely concerned w/my
safety, explained of other marriages.

In spite of his suspicions and concerns, Edmondson agreed with Rose to buy a $62,000 house with three bedrooms and one-and-a-half baths at 3430 This-A-Way Lane N.W in the Lake Symington neighborhood west of Bremerton. It was a long step up from the tiny dwelling she shared with Dugeno and the shabby Long Lake Road house she inherited from Erickson. In such a short time, her talents in the land of opportunity had elevated her to a middle class neighborhood.

She told the Realtor that money for the down payment would come from her ex-husband, but she didn't identify which ex-husband she meant, Dugeno or Manthie. It's likely that by this time, nothing would have remained from Dugeno's estate, and Manthie certainly didn't have the money. Just to be prudent, she also persuaded her new husband to buy mortgage insurance to ensure that if anything happened to him, the mortgage would be paid off.

And after another trip to Montana to visit Manthie in prison, she tried to convince Edmondson that as newlyweds they should buy two $150,000 life insurance policies, with her as the beneficiary of his and him as the beneficiary of hers. Edmondson balked at first, but on September 21, an agent of the Sunset Life Insurance Company went to Rose's house on Long Lake Road and wrote up the policies.

The agent said it was the easiest policy he ever sold and that Rose appeared to be the prime mover behind the idea. It became an office joke, he added, that she wanted it for her husband.

By this time rumors about Rose were circulating widely among sailors– that she'd had five previous husbands, that they'd all ended up dead or missing, that she was collecting life insurance on them. There was some exaggeration here, but there was enough truth to these rumors to make them credible. By now Edmondson knew the rumors too and planned to stop the paperwork on the house he was buying with Rose; he finally accepted the idea that Rose was plotting to kill him for the life insurance and the new house.

"Bill and Rose fought pretty much from day one," said Bill's friend Cogswell. "A lot about money. How she didn't know the value of money. Bill told me she would go out and drink to excess and come home drunk. And I guess her doctor told her she had to cut down on her drinking or it could kill her eventually." At the same time, his friends acknowledged that Edmondson couldn't always be relied on for the truth. "Yeah," said one. "I don't know if you'd call it lies or not. But he was a bullshitter."

While Edmondson was in the hospital recovering from his Tylenol-induced episode of the night of August 28, a sailor named Jerry Dyke called the Security Police at the Bangor Submarine Base to report that Rosalina Edmondson had defrauded him out of a $161 government payroll check. Around mid day August 30, he said, Rose showed up in his room at the submarine base and asked if he wanted to go with her to the Kitsap County Fair that afternoon. Dyke told her he had only a five dollar bill and the payroll check, but Rose said she would cover the costs for the day, so they left for the fair, stopping first at the Sandpiper Restaurant in Silverdale. When Dyke protested, saying he couldn't afford to eat there, Rose said she would treat him to lunch. The bill for lunch and drinks was $19, but Rose said she didn't have enough cash and suggested that Dyke endorse the check over to her and she'd pay the bill. He agreed, but the restaurant wouldn't accept the payroll check so Rose wrote a personal check for the meal and told Dyke she needed the meal money back by Monday or her account would be overdrawn. So they drove to Harrison Hospital where Rose bought Dyke a cup of coffee, then looked for a co-worker and a $20 loan. Thirty minutes later she returned with $20 and she and Dyke went to the fair.

They spent about $20 at the fair, and when they returned to the base Dyke asked for his $161 check. Rose told him she'd cashed it at the hospital and given $100 of it to co-workers to whom she owed money, so Dyke asked for the remaining $61, and Rose said she'd reimburse him on her next payday. Dyke, apparently uninformed about how Rose operated, wasn't sure if she'd cashed the check or signed it over to someone else.

Just before midnight on September 4, Rose was brought in for questioning by the Subase Security Police. Before the interview had barely begun, before any question was put to her, Rose said, "I just don't have time to change my last name yet, because I've been busy working over at the hospital, and I don't have time to change all my last name and stuff yet. I'm going to do it this week. My driver's license has to be changed to this last name [Edmondson]. I just got divorced and got married again."

The investigator got her a cup of coffee, then began getting a display of Rose's mind at work.

"Okay," he began, "You are suspected of taking some money that belonged to another person in the form of a U.S. government check."

"What does that mean?" Rose answered, although nobody ever said she had trouble understanding English.

When investigator put the question a different way, Rose replied, "Oh, yeah!"

Taken aback, the investigator reminded her of her constitutional rights, told her that she didn't have to answer any questions, and that anything she said could be used against her in a trial. She pretended not to understand but then said she was willing to discuss the alleged theft.

In response to a question about where her husband was—by this time Edmondson had been released from the hospital—she said he's not around right now, that he's probably downtown someplace, that it's hard to get a hold of him. She acknowledged meeting Jerry Dyke in his room, showering there, changing clothes, then going to the fair with the $161 check in her purse.

"I know him for a long time," she said of Dyke. "Since he got here. We've been good friends."

"About how long?"

"About two months."

The investigator established that Rose had just married the preceding Friday but that she hadn't officially changed her name yet. He got Rose's permission to search her purse where he found a Subase badge even though Rose hadn't worked at the base for about a year. She said she hadn't had time to turn it in.

"Okay, who is Richard Manthie?"

"Oh, that's my ex husband."

"Where's he?"

"Oh, he's someplace."

"Where?"

"Here in Washington."

"Or in Montana?"

"He's back in Montana."

"He is back in Montana."

"We haven't contact so …"

"What does he do in Montana?"

"He's working back there."

"What kind of work does he do?"

"I don't know, sir. We haven't any contact."

"What is his address in Montana?"

Rose finally acknowledged that Manthie was in prison.

Later in the interview the investigator returned to the subject of Rose's relationship with Jerry Dyke.

"Yeah," she said, "I don't think that Bill know that me and him is good friends, you know. He come down to our house, you know, and have a drink and stuff and I fix him dinner. You know, that's what I do"

"Is that you and your husband that Jerry visited at your house?"

"No, just me. He [Edmondson] don't want him at my house. He don't want to talk to him."

"What's the matter? Don't they get along?"

"Yeah, they don't get along."

"What boat is your husband on?"

"Oh, he's on *Lofan, Levin*, something like that. You know, I don't think Jerry will get that thing stuck to me because I've been really nice to him. Every time he says, 'Rose, you know, we could go someplace else and stuff,' you know. He says, Come on down.' I come down and pick him up, and like Sunday, we went to the fairgrounds and stuff."

"Well, where was your husband?"

"He's in the hospital."

"He was in the hospital while you were at the fairgrounds."

"Yeah, I told him that I'm going to the fairgrounds with this guy. He said, 'That's okay, honey.' He said, 'You have fun' and stuff. Bill's very understandable."

"You told your husband that you were going to the fair?"

"Yeah. He's in the hospital at the time because his lung collapsed. He just got sick. He's not supposed to take Tylenol. He's allergic with it. And took Tylenol."

The conversation circled back to the stop at the Sandpiper restaurant, Rose saying that before she and Dyke went to the fair she had three drinks and Dyke had two. She said Dyke gave her the $161 check at the restaurant, although earlier she said she gave it to her in his room before they left for the restaurant.

"You know," Rose said then, "me and Jerry is really good friends. I don't even think he'll do this to me. If he didn't have no money, he come down and call me. He say, 'Could we go out, you know, and have a good time, dancing and stuff?' I say, 'Alright,' you know. I spent my own money. Because he's a good friend."

The investigator asked her again about her marriages.

"What happened to your first husband?"

"Oh, he passed away. He got a liver problem."

"Did Jerry know you were going to get married?"

"Yeah, he knows. Just said, 'Congratulations,' you know. I just can't believe he did this to me. You know, being nice to a guy and just turn around and did this to you."

Next the investigator asked her about the value of the house she inherited from Erickson.

"Oh, it's about $150,000." (The court had valued it at a third that amount.) As the interview was nearing the end, the investigator asked again about the house Rose inherited from Erickson.

"He gave it to me because my belated husband [Dugeno] and him are really good buddies in the shipyard and really good friends. I don't know. It's like a soap opera."

The 56-minute interview ended at 12:31 AM, September 5, with Rose concerned about having been gone so long. The investigator offered to explain it to her husband.

"Yes, please, cause he got a high temper. Me and him are going to have a big fight tonight. I have to pick him up and I didn't show up."

The investigator reminded her that she said she didn't know where her husband was.

Later, when Rose was officially charged with the theft of Dyke's $161 check, investigators found that she had not cashed the check to pay back another hospital employee as she claimed but instead deposited it in her bank account.

* * *

That September, another sailor had an experience familiar to that of many others who'd met Rose. He'd known her for about a year, he said, when she invited him to her house on Long Lake Road for drinks and dinner. He stayed the night, as other men had, and after leaving the next morning he discovered $900 missing from his pants pocket. He confronted Rose; she denied all knowledge of the money. A verbal fight followed, but the sailor left without his money, and he never reported the theft, he said, partly because he felt foolish about having been taken, partly because he was already on work release from the Kitsap County jail and was trying to avoid additional contact with the law.

That same month, Rose was in the bar of another club at Bangor submarine base where she approached a sailor and asked him to dance. They danced to a couple of tunes when the sailor excused himself to the bathroom, leaving some cash on the bar – one $10 bill, a five and three ones -with instructions to the bartender to buy Rose a drink. When he returned, the 10 and the five were gone, and so was Rose. Navy police interviewed her; Rose denied taking the $15 and said that the sailor was accusing her falsely, out of anger for her looking at another man. No further action was taken.

The Edmondsons closed the deal on the house in the first week of November. Until then Edmondson and his friend Mike Cogswell had been living in the Kariotis apartment, but when the Edmondsons moved into their new house, Cogswell moved in with them, saying that Edmondson wanted him along as a body guard, a development Rose wasn't happy about.

The week of November 13-15, Edmondson made several alarming entries in his journal.

Night of 13 Nov. '81. Left work feeling sick, probably a cold. Rose gave me two large orange/white capsules. I took them and went to bed. About ½ hr. later, very sick, throwing up blood, head fuzzy, vision blurred.

Believe (actually certain) drugged again, same symptoms as when hospitalized late August. Other occurrences out of ordinary happened that night. Woke up next morning in bathtub full of blood, hands + feet tied together with phone cord. Subsequent looking found cord in cabinet missing. Should talk to phone co. about Rose getting new cord when phone finally installed. Rose tied myself up and left in bathtub of cold water. Phone cord around my neck. Still bleeding from head.

Week of 15 Nov. (cont) Checked into motel approx. 2 A.M. 14 Nov. '81. Rose left @ approx. 7:30 A.M., said for about ½ hr., returned approx. approx. 17-18 hrs. later. Said was waiting for brother. Probably seeing Richard. Very suspicious.

Week of Nov. 14 '81. On making trip to Montana, called Richard Manthie, ex-husb. Said he is still in prison will be paroled. Stated there due to lies, didn't go further. Said Rose was there around September 7 @ visited (no reason). On way there, would not say where going + would not turn back, although I demanded it.

23 Nov 81 Did not return home. No calls or explanation for this.

24 Nov 81 – Received call. Did not get to phone in time. Hung up.

24 Nov 81 – Evening, returned home from walk. Rose not home. Rose called @ approx. 7:30 P.M. stating @ Joyce's house, car broken. Said Joyce will bring her home. Never came home that night.

On another page headed "<u>MISC. NOTES</u>," undated but probably written at about this time, he wrote, *"Insurance beneficiary to be changed on policy and SGIT [Service members Group Life Insurance]. All things to go elsewhere (home – PA).*

Rose made another trip to Deer Lodge where she aggressively advocated for Manthie's parole, saying she'd guarantee him a place to stay at her house on Long Lake Road in Port Orchard and that she'd have employment for him.

In early December, she changed her last name from Edmondson to Manthie on the payroll records at Harrison Hospital, even though she was married to Edmondson and divorced Manthie earlier in the year. When she talked with Manthie's parole officer in Port Orchard, she told him she was Rosalina Manthie.

On the 12th of December Rose made the first payment on the $150,000 life insurance policies but her check bounced. Five days later Rose mailed a money order for the payment due on the insurance, and that same day Manthie was paroled from the state prison in Montana, having served less than one year of his five-year sentence. This man, erroneously judged to be a non-violent offender, was released into Rose's supervision.

Official reports on his stay in Deer Lodge indicate that his adjustment to prison was satisfactory. He earned a GED, maintained a steady work record, and participated in several therapy classes. On his exit interview he said he'd been convicted unjustly of a burglary that never happened. "Did you learn anything from your incarceration?" he was asked. "I didn't learn a shitting thing," he replied. Did he benefit from the therapy classes? "I got out a lot of anger and learned how to deal with liars."

Rose paid for his flight to Seattle and met him at the airport where they spent the night in a nearby motel, then returned with him to her house on Long Lake Road in Port Orchard. He settled in there while Rose was nominally living with Edmondson at Lake Symington.

On the afternoon of Monday, December 21st, the date Edmondson would become a missing person, Rose accompanied Manthie as he checked in with his parole officer. He then drove Rose to work at the hospital before returning to Long Lake Road.

When Edmondson failed to show up for work on December 22, Cogswell finally reached Rose at work. She told him the same story she'd told the detectives, about Edmondson meeting a longhaired guy at the Sea Deck Restaurant and leaving to get drugs. Cogswell was suspicious; while he'd known Rose to use drugs, he had never seen Edmondson do it. It was the false scent she left for Magerstaedt.

Rose never came home to Lake Symington the night of Tuesday the 22nd, and so when Cogswell next saw her it was Wednesday. "She was pretty much he same," he said, "but she kept bringing up the insurance. It seemed really mysterious. She seemed more concerned about making the monthly payment than if Bill ever came back or not. She kept saying, 'What am I going to do? What am I going to do? With all these bills. How am I ever going to pay all these bills?'"

The next payment on the house wasn't due until January 1, Cogswell said. Edmondson had told Cogswell he had just enough money to make the payment, but he said he didn't expect the marriage to last until Christmas, that he was tired of Rose never being around, and that he was talking about moving back into the Navy barracks. "The main reason he was going to stay," Cogswell explained, "was to find out why she was trying to poison him. I think he wanted to catch her in the act and be a hero."

Meanwhile Manthie continued his reckless ways. At 2:00 PM on December 28, just a few days after being released from prison and the day before Edmondson's body was found, he was pulled over by a Port Orchard police officer on suspicion of drunk driving. While the officer was looking at Manthie's military I.D., Manthie grabbed it out of his hands and the two scuffled over it. Two additional officers arrived to help subdue him, cuff him, and take him to a holding cell at the county jail where he was charged with DWI, obstructing a public servant, and driving without a valid license. They found he had seven $100 bills in his possession, an unusual sum for a man just released from prison.

It was an inauspicious but predictable beginning to his life as a parolee.

He calmed down after half an hour, explained that he'd just been released from prison in Montana, gave the name of his parole officer, and said he could pay the $937 in bail money if he could just make some phone calls. When he reached Rose, she said she'd come with the money.

The Investigation

December 29, 1981—June 14, 1982

At 10:00 PM the day Edmondson's body was discovered, while Magerstaedt was still interviewing Rose at the Sheriff's office, Morgan drove to Rose's house on Long Lake Road in South Kitsap, a house detectives described as a dump, cluttered, a dwelling that must have been hard to heat in winter. Manthie was there, having been bailed out of jail by Rose, and they showed him the permission form Rose had signed. "Go ahead, help yourself," Manthie said.

The '73 Gremlin two-door hatchback was tomato soup red with a white stripe along each side and was covered with frost. Even at night they could see that the inside of the car had been freshly painted black. It was still tacky to the touch.

From the floor behind the driver's seat they recovered a pair of scissors with red spots on the blades, a baseball cap with red stains on it, and dirt and fabric samples from the floor in front of the driver's seat. They also noted some reddish spots near the door handle on one side.

They went indoors to talk, and the detectives told Manthie about his Constitutional rights. The best he could remember about the night of December 21st, Manthie said, was that Rose drove to the house about 11:30 or midnight, that she was not drunk, that she stayed all night and left in the morning.

He admitted they argued, mostly about his drinking: Rose was concerned that he couldn't care for their three-year-old daughter when he was drunk.

Did they sleep together that night, the detectives asked? Manthie wouldn't answer the question.

What kind of shoes do you wear, Morgan asked? Manthie pointed to the work boots he had on. These are all I ever wear, he said. "I looked around though," Morgan wrote in his report "and behind the stove I saw a fairly nice pair of cowboy boots. I did not mention these at the time."

Manthie said he didn't know Rose all that well and wasn't sure what she'd been up to, that he really didn't care about all her boyfriends, they didn't bother him.

Had he ever seen her with a gun? Yes, he gave her a gun two to three years earlier, a 9mm, because she'd been the victim of a robbery and he didn't want that to happen again, and she probably hadn't mentioned it because he was on parole at the time.

Tell us about the fresh paint in the car. The Gremlin. "Oh, that's always been that way since we got it."

How'd you get those bruises on your knuckles? "Working on cars," he said. "Hoisting an engine. Scraped my knuckles.'

And what do you do for a living? He cut wood for the neighbors, he said. He didn't need much because he didn't have to pay child support, he explained, and the house [the house Rose inherited from Erickson] would be part his as soon as probate was settled. He didn't know that Rose had divorced him.

As the conversation went on, Manthie changed his story about Rose staying the night, saying that sometime during the night Rose got up, that he thought she went next door to the home of Ken and Mayselle Davis, which could barely be seen through the trees, but the next morning the car was gone and Manthie assumed she'd gone to work.

At 9:00 the next morning, December 30, Morgan and Magerstaedt drove to Long Lake Road to talk with 52-year-old Mayselle Davis, the next door neighbor, to see what they could learn about Rose and Manthie. When they approached the Davis house, Rose's car was parked in the driveway but when they went inside they didn't see her. Davis said she hurried into the bedroom when she saw the detectives coming. Rather than interview Davis with Rose in the next room, the detectives drove her to the sheriff's office to talk.

In spite of having cared for Valery off and on – she felt more like a mother to the girl than a babysitter – Mayselle Davis knew surprisingly little about her neighbors next door. She didn't know that Rose had divorced Manthie while he was in prison, for example, or that Rose had already married again. And because Rose kept Edmondson away from her life on Long Lake Road, Davis knew nothing of him.

Feeling freer to talk at the sheriff's office, Davis told the detectives that at about 12:30 that morning she heard a knock at her bedroom window.

70

It was Rose, calling her "Mom" and asking to be let in. She was dressed in a faded pink bathrobe and sock-type slippers. She was crying and had a swollen nose, the result, Rose said, of a blow from Manthie. To escape from him, she said, she had to jump out a window. During a half-hour conversation, Davis inferred that Rose and Manthie had fought over Rose having other boyfriends. If Manthie had known that Rose not only had other boyfriends but a new husband, her injuries might have been much worse.

Rose spent the night on Davis's couch but when Davis got up about 7:00, Rose was gone, so Davis walked to Rose's house where she saw a door to the house had been broken off its hinges and was resting against the jamb, and that glass in the door was broken and scattered about the floor. Davis told the detectives that Rose claimed to have locked Manthie out and that he'd broken down the door. Davis said she'd seen a fresh cut on his hand.

Later that morning, around 11:00, Magerstaedt arrived at the sheriff's office with Richard Manthie and three-year-old Valery, who'd spent most of the two preceding years at the Davis house. Davis left with Valery, and Manthie, having been read his Constitutional rights, agreed to talk with Morgan and Magerstaedt.

Fresh from prison, he said he didn't want to make any trouble and was happy to help in any way he could. But in answering questions about the night of December 21st he appeared to have a clouded memory and was vague in many of his answers, partly because he was drunk enough that night to get the car stuck in the ditch.

But he remembered working around the yard the next morning, going to the Davis house around noon, coming home and working on the pickup, drinking a beer, calling his probation officer, and going to see him at 3:00. He returned home, he said, worked on his chain saw until evening, then went back to the Davis house and drank beer until he got "pretty drunk." Rose called him there, wanting to talk with him at home, so he walked through the trees to her house where they got into an argument about his drinking and his inability to care for their child when he was drunk. Then, he said, Rose walked out the door and left.

Davis said Rose returned the next morning, the 31st, so she went to Rose's house to talk with Rose and Manthie, who said they were going to get their troubles straightened out. Davis stayed for a while and she and Manthie drank beer and got drunk.

Morgan asked him about the fresh paint inside the
Gremlin. It was that way when he returned from prison in Montana on the 19th, Manthie said, and that as far as he knew it was that way when Rose bought it.

And the cut on his hand? He cut it while working on a car, he said.

He said it was on the night of the 21st when he learned from Rose that she was married to somebody named William and that this William had never been to her house on Long Lake Road, at least as far as he knew. At the end of this conversation with Morgan and Magerstaedt, Manthie agreed to allow a search of the house for evidence but stipulated that the search be limited to things that might be connected to the homicide, explaining that he didn't know what kinds of narcotics Rose might have around the house.

When Morgan drove Manthie home, he asked again about the fresh paint in the Gremlin and Manthie replied as he had before and added, "You can look at anything on the property." In the car Morgan noticed what he thought was blood but said nothing, then they went inside to talk.

Obviously there was a door here, Morgan said. What happened to it?

Manthie explained that they were short on firewood that he'd broken it down for burning. Had there been a window in the door? No, Manthie said.

But when Morgan told him he knew about the fight and Manthie's breaking down the door, Manthie admitted it.

Other detectives arrived to search the house for evidence while Morgan continued his conversation with Manthie, who said he knew what Rose had done before she came home the night of the 21st. She had many boyfriends and could have done anything with them. She was a heavy drug user, he said, and these boy friends often stayed at the house and "kept things there."

Magerstaedt noted that Manthie wore a wedding ring. Manthie explained that he still loved Rose but said, " I thought it would be easier to pick up girls if they thought I was married." He denied having any kind of affair with Rose after she married Edmondson, said they were just friends and talked about remodeling the house.

Magerstaedt checked inside the Gremlin and also thought he saw blood running down the passenger seat, so he asked Manthie to look at it. Did Manthie know what that was? Manthie wasn't sure. "It looks like blood to me," Magerstaedt said. "It looks like something," Manthie replied. Manthie gave permission to impound the car and the car was taken to the sheriff's office for examination.

By the time the crime scene investigators were done inside, they had taken 15 photos, including photos of blood spots on the floor and the doorjamb and one of a pistol case on a dresser. They also gathered several pieces of physical evidence: Pieces of glass off the floor, scrapings of two different blood spots, two cotton balls stained with blood, and the bag from the vacuum cleaner.

At the funeral home, they took hair samples from Edmondson's head, chest, and pubic area.

That same day, two other detectives, returned to the tree farm where Edmondson's body was found and took a plaster cast of the boot print found earlier.

It was a perfect match with the boots they'd borrowed from Manthie. Cogswell had cowboy boots too and said Rose stole his boots from him and took them to her lawyer in an attempt to depict Cogswell as the murderer, but the boots were the wrong size. The detectives also placed a photo of the tires on the 1973 red AMC Gremlin along side the tire tracks at the scene. The tracks matched those in the photo.

Before the detectives left, Manthie told Morgan that if he were charged with murder he'd serve a lot of time, a life sentence. "Well, maybe 10 years," Morgan said. "Oh, no," Manthie replied, "they'll bitch me 'cause this is my third felony conviction."

Late the afternoon of the 30th, Morgan and Magerstaedt drove to see 28-year-old Mike Cogswell, the sailor who lived with the Edmondsons in the split-level house they'd just bought on This-A-Way Lane west of Bremerton. Cogswell confirmed some of what the detectives had heard before – that on the afternoon of the 21st he and Edmondson were drinking beer at the house when Rose came home. Edmondson was angry that Rose hadn't been home so he and Cogswell went to the Union Tavern to drink beer and shoot pool. When they got home, Rose was still there, and Bill was well on his way to intoxication.

The newlyweds went out together that evening, an unusual event, Cogswell said, leaving in Rose's red Gremlin, and they didn't return that night. When Cogswell finally reached Rose at work the next day, she denied not coming home, but he saw that their bed hadn't been slept in. She told him her story, well rehearsed by now, about Edmondson meeting some bearded guy at the Sea Deck Restaurant and going off with him to get some acid, leaving her alone. Cogswell asked if she'd left the outside light on when she left for work at 4:00 AM on the 21st, knowing she hadn't. When she said yes, he knew she was lying again.

From Cogswell, the detectives learned that Edmondson and his wife argued frequently, that Edmondson believed she was trying to kill him, that she sometimes disappeared for three to four days at a time, and that Edmondson was missing a $1,500 watch and some stereo equipment that Cogswell suspected she'd stolen and sold. Edmondson had closed out his checking account on December 19th, two days before he died, preferring to carry cash because Rose always overdrew funds, and he was carrying $200 in cash the night he disappeared, money that was not in his pockets when his body was found.

Cogswell also told them that Edmondson said she carried a pistol in her purse, that she told her husband not to come to her house on Long Lake Road, a fact that puzzled him because they were buying the house on This-A-Way, and that he, not Rose, reported his friend missing when he didn't show up at work on the morning of December 22nd. Rose was concerned mostly about how she was going to make the house payment.

76

Edmondson owed Cogswell money from the time they lived together before Edmondson married, so he let Cogswell live with them until that debt was repaid, an arrangement that greatly displeased Rose. His room was across the hall from theirs.

About a week before his death, Edmondson told his friend that Naval Investigative Services and local civilian police suspected she'd murdered previous husbands or boyfriends. Edmondson confronted her about it one night, asking about some papers he found in the house with the name "Mark" on them and about the disappearance of $3,000. They got in another fight and Rose disappeared again for three or four days. He finally went looking for her but couldn't find her. "That last week, Thursday," Cogswell said, "he thought he had it all figured out. Well, she never came back that Friday, or Saturday, or Sunday. When we got back to the house Monday night, she was there. And then her and Bill went out that night, and that's the last time I seen him." He was referring to the night of Monday, December 21st, the night Edmondson disappeared.

The day after Edmondson didn't show up for work, Cogswell, remembering his friend's concern about being killed, began making phone calls, and when he finally reached Rose at the hospital late that afternoon, she told the story about the Sea Deck Restaurant, the bearded man, and Edmondson's going with him to get drugs, a story he never believed. As skeptical as he was about some of his friend's stories, he was infinitely more skeptical about Rose.

When Cogswell next saw Rose, she was unconcerned about her husband but terribly concerned about money. He told the detectives again how she kept bringing up the insurance and didn't seem concerned about Bill's disappearance.

He explained that the money for the down payment may have come from a Joyce Elton, one of Rose's co-workers at the hospital and that the first payment on the mortgage was due on January 1. "Bill had taken out an advance and had just enough money to make the first payment, but he told me a couple of weeks ago he didn't think he'd be staying around, that the marriage wouldn't last 'til Christmas. He said, 'I'm not going to take this, her not being around. I'm not going to take this. I'm going back to the barracks.' The main reason he stayed was to find out why she was trying to poison him. And, uh, kill him or something."

Morgan asked about this poisoning attempt. "The first time was about a month ago. When we were living in the Kariotis Apartments on Athens Way. I remember Rose saying, 'I'll take care of you. I'll take care of you.' Then I remember his being in the hospital and being tested for drugs in his system, some drug you can only get in the Philippines or something. I don't know if that's true or not.

"Another time he supposedly slipped in the bath tub and smashed the back of his head up. I seen it. It was all scraped up. Later he said he thought he was drugged up. He said some guy was there too,

and they were trying to hit him over the head with
something."

Morgan questioned him about Rose's
allegations of a homosexual relationship but
Cogswell affirmed that both he and Edmondson were
straight and acknowledged that he also had had sex
with Rose while she was going out with Edmondson.

He told Morgan about sailors she's gone out
with and who'd found money or checks missing, and
about friends who urged Edmondson to have the
marriage annulled before something happened. He
told about Edmondson never having been to the
house Rose inherited from Erickson, the house on
Long Lake Road, because Rose wouldn't give him a
key, and about Edmondson being puzzled that she
wouldn't bring the furniture and the television from
that house to the new house they were buying. "Bill
could never figure that out," he said.

But Cogswell did go out to that house, he
said, on the Wednesday, two days after his friend
didn't show up for work, and Rose's Monza was
there, even though she told him it was in a garage
being repaired.

"I knocked on the door, and I asked for Rose,
and a guy comes to the door, and I asked, 'Rose
here?' and he said, 'No,' and I said, 'Who are you?'
and he said, 'Well, I'm Rich, I'm her husband.'
That's what he said: 'I'm her husband.' So I said,
'You didn't know she got remarried?' and he said,
'No, we filed, she filed for divorce, but I was in

prison.' I asked him if he knew a Bill Edmondson and he said he didn't. I described him and he said he didn't even know she got remarried."

At the end of his interview with Morgan, Cogswell added that, Yes, he thought he remembered there being glass in the door Manthie said he broke up for firewood, the door Manthie said had no window.

Detective Morgan also interviewed John Michael Niles, Edmondson's immediate Navy superior, who claimed he knew the victim as well as anybody else in the squadron. Niles confirmed Cogswell's reports about the fights about money between Rose and Edmondson and said that she often went out alone and came home drunk, adding that her doctor warned her that her heavy drinking could kill her.

Niles was able to provide more details about the first time Edmondson thought he'd been poisoned. He said Cogswell returned from Seattle to the apartment he and Edmondson shared and found the place torn up and furniture thrown out the window. Edmondson was gone so Cogswell called Niles and next day called the police. Two people had been in there fighting, he learned, and one was arrested. Edmondson had gone berserk and was running around the apartment nude, throwing things out the windows and tearing things up.

He was in the hospital for about a week but wasn't sure what had happened to him. He suspected she'd slipped an overdose of Tylenol in his drink, knowing he was allergic to Tylenol. When he was interviewed under hypnosis by a Navy psychiatrist, he said the last thing he could remember before passing out was Rose sitting on his chest and pushing pills down his throat.

Niles said Edmondson had heard the rumors that Rose had five previous husbands who turned up dead or mysteriously missing and that she was collecting life insurance, and like Cogswell, he said Edmondson was trying to stop the purchase of the house on This-A-Way.

Had Niles ever been to Rose's house on Long Lake Road? "Yeah, after Bill and Rose were married. We went out there to look for her, but she wasn't there. Some guy named Mark was there, and he said, 'This is my house. I'm living here.' He kicked us out." Niles was probably referring to Mark Johnson, the live-in boyfriend who had returned to Albuquerque.

Niles said he'd ridden in the Gremlin once or twice. It wasn't in very good shape, he said. And no, there was no fresh paint or any smell of fresh paint.

Later that night Ray Magerstaedt received a call from Allen Brown, a former of security guard at Harrison Hospital. Brown had read the news story about the murder and drew a connection between Rose and the murder, and having talked with her often, knew that Rose had a .22, either a rifle or a pistol, and that to ward off prowlers she kept it at the house she inherited from Erickson. She also told him that she'd been married several times, once to get into this country.

In an 11-page handwritten statement, Brown said Rose told him she was afraid of Manthie because he had beat her up and because he had killed a man once by kicking and stomping him to death, a partial description of the killing of Bill Edmondson. Brown also said that Bob Erickson, his good friend and the man Rose had befriended shortly before his death, didn't want to leave his house to his wife's three children, so Brown suggested he leave it to Rose, and Erickson liked the idea because it would make a nice home for her daughter Valery.

The night before Erickson's death, Brown ran into him in the hospital parking lot and noted that Erickson was in good sprits. He had just bought a new tail light for his car, and although he'd had heart problems, his doctor had just told him he was doing well. He showed Brown a prescription the doctor had given him for digitoxin, a drug administered for people with heart problems but when used in an overdose can cause a heart attack. Agatha Christie also used digitoxin as a murder weapon in "Appointment With Death."

Rose told Brown that her husband, Richard Manthie, just came back from Montana and that the two of them had gone together to see Erickson. Brown noted in his report that Erickson didn't show up for work the next day, which was not like him. He reached Rose by phone; Rose said she had seen him just last night and he was okay. But then Brown received a call from one of Erickson's stepchildren: Erickson was dead. She had found him in his bed, soaking wet. The house was a mess, she said, with the front door unlocked.

Brown called Rose again right away to report Erickson's death but she didn't seem shocked or upset, and he felt she was changing her story about having gone to see Erickson with Manthie. A few days later, she said to Brown that she had told Erickson's ghost to go back where he came from. She added that Erickson had wanted to die and be with his wife, a claim that wasn't believable to Brown because Erickson had just completed a boiler tender course at Tacoma Community College and was also enjoying his job as a security officer at the hospital.

Rose told Brown she had trouble with prowlers at the house on Long Lake Road and that someone had gone through the box where Erickson kept his stock and bond certificates but nothing was missing. She told him she wanted to get a gun, a little derringer, and a week later she told him she had bought what he thought was a .22 pistol.

Later Rose approached Brown to request a $200 loan to repair damage Manthie did to her car, damage her insurance didn't cover. Brown declined. In his statement he wrote that as a hospital security officer he had written up Rose for a fight with another Filipino employee in the kitchen, and that another employee had written her up for an alleged theft of money from the billfold of a hospital visitor.

Brown wrote that around mid March 1982, two and a half months after Edmondson's death, he had another conversation with Rose at the hospital.

"Have you heard what happened?" she asked cheerfully. "My husband was killed."

Brown put the question to her: Did Richard do it? Kill your husband?

Rose hesitated, then didn't answer.

Brown asked again.

"No," she said. "Richard said he loved me, but not enough to kill anyone for me."

Rose told Brown that Erickson's three step children had set Richard up as the killer and implied that they had something to do with Edmondson's death. One of Erickson's sons had been picked up for drunken driven and was placed in the same cell as Manthie, she claimed, and told Manthie that Erickson and Rose had been sleeping together, and maybe Erickson's heart just couldn't take it. Or maybe he died from poison after his recent operation.

She claimed her husband must have been mugged because when he was found, he had no money or jewelry on him, facts she couldn't have known.

Rose must have realized she was a suspect in Edmondson's death: Her boss and four other cafeteria employees had been subpoenaed. Besides, she told Brown in a conversation at his table in the cafeteria, "Bob Erickson's stepchildren want me to run. I'm scared for my life. If you help me out of this, I'll give you [Erickson's] house." Again Brown declined. Oddly, the last thing she said before walking away from his table: "They have thieves and murderers working here."

Another hospital worker, Wes Niquette, described her as "a good little worker" who washed dishes, prepared simple foods, served food, wiped down tables, and generally filled in for other employees. "A nice person," he said. "She was very, very thin," he added, "with long black hair, and she had one front tooth outlined in gold or silver. By my standards, she wasn't particularly attractive." Her appearance began to deteriorate after Edmondson's death, he said; she neglected personal hygiene and became erratic in her attendance at work, phoning in sick or just not showing up, drinking a lot under the cloud of suspicion.

Niquette spoke favorably of Manthie, though, describing him as a willing worker who showed no intolerance of authority and who may have found some comfort in the orderly routine of a job where he didn't have to make decisions, where other people relieved him of that responsibility. When Manthie was arrested and extradited to Montana on charges of burglary and rape, Niquette and other hospital employees were stunned.

The detectives also talked with Joyce Elton, Rose's 55-year-old close friend through the hospital who told them that Rose kept a hand gun in her glove compartment, and that she knew both Edmondson and Manthie.

* * *

Cogswell informed the detectives that it was Rose, not Edmondson, who'd made the down payment on the $60,000 house on This-A-Way, and that she wanted the house to come to her if anything happened to her husband. They hadn't even made the first payment on the mortgage.

When Cogswell had a chance to look inside the Gremlin, he said it was much cleaner than usual, there being no tapes, coffee cups and other trash littering the floor, and the inside door panels and the backs of the front seats were cleaner than he remembered.

And when detectives took Edmondson's blue running shoes from the evidence bag and examined the soles with a magnifying glass, they saw what they believed to be shards of glass. Other information, varying in value, began coming in by phone. An insurance company called to report that a Rosaline Edmondson had recently bought a policy that would pay off the mortgage in case of death.

Two hours later Cogswell called to say he'd gone to the house on This-A-Way to pick up some clothes and saw that Edmondson's navy blue jacket was gone, a jacket with "Sub Squadron 17" in white letters on the chest.

A neighbor on Long Lake Road who'd read news reports called to say he and his wife were awakened about 3:00 AM December 22nd or 23rd by five rapid pistol shots from somewhere nearby.

Cogswell remembered that Edmondson wore two rings on his ring finger, one a plain gold band he'd bought at a discount store in Bremerton, the other a gold-colored ring with four or five "diamonds" across the top that he bought at half price at the Navy Exchange. It was too big so he wrapped gray tape around the bottom and put the plain band on afterward to keep the "diamond ring" from slipping off.

Neither ring was on Edmondson when his body was found, just a band of pale skin where rings had been.

By the end of the day December 31st, just two days after Bill Edmondson's body was found, naval investigators and the sheriff's office were exchanging information and the pieces were coming together.

The Investigation, Continued

January 1, 1982

Dave Morgan couldn't have celebrated too hard – he was in the office New Year's Day making phone calls to a Vernon Marion, the man who sold the Gremlin to Rose some time in October for $475, the money put up by "an older white woman," undoubtedly Rose's friend Joyce Elton. No, Marion said, the inside of the car hadn't been painted when he sold it.

Had he ever seen Rose or Edmondson with a gun? "Well, Bill had talked about owning a .44 mag pistol and a 357 pistol, but then he also said that Edmondson was a bull shitter." On the other hand, he said, "Bill gave one of those pistols as payment for the car."

The next day, detectives took a call from a man whose wife worked in the hospital kitchen with Rose. The wife said that shortly after Edmondson disappeared, Rose came to work "beat to hell with a black eye and bruises." She also said that Rose was very friendly with "a long haired, very dirty man," a description that might have fit Manthie, but then she was friendly with many other men.

Two days later Detective Magerstaedt made two productive calls, the first to the insurance agent who sold the life policy to the Edmondsons. There were two policies, the agent, explained, each for $150,000, one on Rose with her daughter Valery as the beneficiary, the other on Edmondson with Rose as the lucky winner. The agent said it was the easiest policy he ever sold.

In a call to the Connecticut Insurance Company, Magerstaedt learned that the mortgage insurance policy the Edmondsons had taken out on the house on This-A-Way hadn't been approved. They also learned that Mrs. Edmondson appeared to be the prime mover in getting the policy and he repeated the office joke about her getting it for her husband.

Morgan went to the Lake Flora Road to examine the chain that blocked the entrance to the tree farm where Edmondson's body had been found. By lifting the metal cable, he saw that even if a short person lifted it, a Gremlin could easily pass underneath. Looking closer, he saw what looked like red paint on the cable so he took the cable as evidence.

The Sheriff's office now had the expertise of investigator Doug Hudson, just returned from vacation. Hudson was a large man, over six feet and about 200 pounds, "a little goofy looking," as one colleague said, who combed his brown hair over a bald spot. He was the best crime scene man in the department and excellent on a witness stand: Precise, well organized, articulate and meticulous. He often walked around the office in a white lab coat.

Using a flashlight, Hudson, looked through the windows on the locked Gremlin that had been brought in as evidence and noticed what looked like blood on the transmission hump and what appeared to be hair on other surfaces of the interior. On the roof and hood of the car were scratches, some side-to-side, others front-to-back. He called for a search warrant to gain access to the interior.

By this time, Rose had retained a lawyer to intervene between her and the sheriff's investigators.

Magerstaedt interviewed five people who had been working at the SeaDeck Restaurant the night of December 21, the night Rose said she and her husband were drinking there, the night Edmondson disappeared, but none could remember seeing either Rose, her husband, or a bearded man.

On January 6, with a search warrant in hand, Morgan led Detective Magerstaedt and other Sheriff's investigators to Rose's house at 2299 Long Lake Road. No one was home so they used a chain cutter to enter through the gate leading to the driveway to house, which wasn't locked. Morgan noted the doorjamb broken in from the outside and small fragments of glass on the floor and hair on the door leading to the upstairs. In the bedroom upstairs that Manthie said was his, there was blood on the mattress and a shotgun case with a little plate bearing Rose's name. In the same room was a zippered, fleece-lined pistol case, empty.

Downstairs, two of the investigators were sifting through ashes in the wood stove and kept what appeared to be a metal snap and the burnt remains of a button. Another spotted a can of black spray paint and took a photo of it.

They went through what appeared to be the main bedroom of the house where they saw men's and women's clothing and a Marine's uniform, spent shotgun shells and a few live ones, costume jewelry, four wristwatches, a man's pocket watch, and two wedding rings, one of them a solid gold band and the other a "man's type ring." The top drawer of a dresser was filled with boxes of condoms.

Outside, several inches of recent snow made it difficult to find evidence, but near one of the outbuildings, on top of the snow, Morgan and Magerstaedt found a pile of fresh ashes containing part of a metal zipper, a buckle, and part of a door that had been burned. When they were done, they left a copy of the warrant in the house and a list of items taken.

January 7, 1981

Detective Morgan reached Edmondson's mother, now Janet Skelton, and her husband Carroll at their home in Moscow, Pennsylvania, and learned from Edmondson's mother that she last talked with her son on December 14. Edmondson called to tell her that Rose had written bad checks and run up bills on the credit card. He stopped payment on her checks she'd written and destroyed the credit cards, so Rose left him, he said.

When Edmondson didn't call his mother on Christmas, as he always did, she tried to call him but Rose answered the phone. Rose told her mother-in-law that Bill had been missing since December 22 and repeated the story about their having gone out drinking that night and about Bill leaving with another man to get drugs. Bill was a heavy drug user and a confirmed liar, Rose said to Bill's mother, claiming he'd said he and his family were wealthy Jews. But Bill had run off now, leaving her behind in the house payment, implying that she could lose the house. It was a clumsy appeal for money.

Edmondson's mother said she'd asked Rose if the couple had received the Christmas package they'd sent, and the $50 money order sent by Edmondson's grandmother. No, Rose said, they hadn't received them.

The conversation moved to the leather jacket Edmondson wore the night he disappeared. Edmondson's mother knew the jacket well, even where it came from – the Burlington Coat Factory near Scranton, PA. She told Morgan she'd check her photo albums and contact the company to find a photograph of the same design.

Edmondson's mother then read to Morgan two letters she received from the Navy, the first one very complimentary about Bill, the second containing allegations about his using drugs. Rose reinforced this allegation in a phone call with Edmondson's mother on January 6, claiming that because she gave information to sheriff's deputies about Bill as a drug user, and because of his association with drug dealers, she was afraid to go to their home on This-A-Way. All Morgan could say was that the investigators knew of no connection between Edmondson and drugs.

How did Bill feel about children, Morgan asked, specifically about three-year-old Valery?

Edmondson's mother recalled that Bill had always been attracted to women with children, that many of his ex-girlfriends had been women with children, adding that he seemed to have much more affection for the child than for his wife Rose.

Interviews of other employees at Harrison Hospital's cafeteria confirmed that Rose was a topic of conversation there, especially Tuesday of the day Edmondson was reported missing and Rose came to work with a black eye. They already knew that Edmondson was missing, and since they knew Manthie from his earlier employment at the hospital, they assumed it was Manthie who delivered the black eye, but, No, Rose insisted, Richard would never do such a thing.

She told another fellow employee that Edmondson kept an axe in his car and that he'd threatened to kill her if he caught her with another man. It was one more trail of crumbs designed to lead detectives away from Richard Manthie.

Her supervisor gave her time off to accompany Edmondson's body back to Pennsylvania, a trip paid for buy her friend Joyce Elton.

When they followed up on Rose's report about the night of December 21, the night she said she and her husband went to Chugwaters to drink and dance, the detectives learned that because the 21st was a Monday night, a football game was on the television so there was no band and no dancing, and even if a Filipino lady had been dancing with a lot of sailors, as Rose claimed, the bartender said she would certainly have noticed. Rose's version of events continued to unravel.

In a visit to the Chief of Military Police at Bangor, Detective Magerstaedt learned that Rose knew that Edmondson was planning to divorce her.

On January 11, Superior Court Judge Leonard Kruse granted the request of Deputy Prosecutor Warren Sharpe and ordered that Richard Manthie submit to blood and hair samples.

On January 13, knowing that Edmondson's funeral had taken place in Pennsylvania, Morgan called Edmondson's mother for a report and heard that Rose had been exceptionally emotional during the service, that she'd wailed and climbed on the casket and torn off the American flag, showing a degree of grief that even the victim's mother thought excessive.

During this visit Rose told her mother-in-law that Bill still owed Mike Cogswell $400 for damage he'd done to his friend's art while rampaging through their apartment and throwing things out windows. Edmondson's mother recognized the poorly disguised invitation to pay the debt, an invitation she declined.

On the afternoon of January 14, the Kitsap County Prosecutor's office was in the process of dictating a warrant for Richard Manthie's arrest, citing the following evidence presented by the detectives: Edmondson's recent marriage with Rose, her purchase of life insurance on Edmondson and mortgage insurance on their new house, Manthie's being in the area at the time of the murder, his criminal background, the boot prints found near the body, the blood found at the Long Lake house matching Edmondson's, the fresh paint in the Gremlin matching the can of spray paint in the house, the scratches in the red paint atop the Gremlin matching the red paint on the chain across the entrance to the tree farm where the body was found, the consistency between a .22 shell found in the car and the wounds on the victim, and the match between the glass fragments found in the soles of the victim's shoes and those found on the floor of the house. Finally there was the victim's diary and the likelihood that the damage done to the victim's body could not have been done by anyone as small as Rose.

When detectives went to Rose's house on Long Lake Road to see her and Manthie, Manthie was just pulling out of the driveway in a 1965 pickup. He stopped at the mailbox, then drove on with the detectives following. He pulled into a Long Lake Texaco station on Highway 16 where they stopped him. Magerstaedt ordered Manthie out of the truck and told him to grasp the bed of the truck while he felt him for weapons and told him he was under arrest for the murder of William H. Edmondson.

He cuffed Manthie, put him into the patrol car without resistance, and read him his rights, which by this time Manthie probably could have recited without a prompt. Magerstaedt asked where Rose was, but Manthie wouldn't answer questions without a lawyer present. He was booked into the Kitsap County Jail with no offer of bail.

A jail sergeant said that while it was common for incarcerated people to be violent, Manthie wasn't much of a management problem. But she added that in her 25 years at the jail, he was "one of the few people who made the hairs stand up on the back of my neck. You'd look into his eyes and there was nothing there. Blank. It was like looking at glass eyes. There was no person inside."

With Manthie secure in jail, the detectives now focused on Rose. Morgan finally located Mark Johnson, Rose's former boyfriend who lived with her for a while on Long Lake Road before he left the Navy and returned to Albuquerque. Johnson couldn't remember with certainty whether Rose had a gun or not. In his last conversation with her, Rose told him she was pregnant and he wanted to know if the child might be his, but given her record with men, it would have been impossible for her to know at that time.

Still seeking information linking Rose to guns, detectives learned that her first husband in this country, the 76-year-old Pete Dugeno, now dead, had a .22 pistol that Rose would have inherited. From the assistant manager of a liquor store, they learned that Rose had given him four guns to sell – a semi-automatic shotgun, a pump action shotgun, a 300 caliber rifle, and a .22 caliber rifle – but that in mid 1981, Rose took them back.

First thing in the morning of January 17, Dave Morgan received another call from Mark Johnson in Albuquerque. Rose called him, he said, to tell him "there had been some trouble up here and that Bill Edmondson was killed in a drug-related murder." She told Johnson she wasn't married to Edmondson because she was still married to Manthie, even though she knew her effort to divorce him was successful in the fall of 1981. Rose told Johnson again that she was pregnant with his child. "If she's pregnant by me," Johnson told Morgan, "she should be due sometime in February." To Morgan, she didn't look eight months along, nor was there was any evidence that she was pregnant then.

He didn't know that Rose had feigned pregnancy to help induce Edmondson to marry her, but Morgan's next contact was Jeanne Marie Lawrence, a 24-year-old woman who'd been close to Manthie during one of his rancorous separations from Rose. They'd lived together from July to November 1980 while Manthie and Rose were separated and their divorce was pending, and she thought about marrying him. She told Morgan that Manthie kept some kind of pistol "under the floorboards" of his car where Rose couldn't find it; he was afraid of what Rose might do with it.

Lawrence visited Manthie in jail where he insisted that neither he nor Rose had anything to do with Edmondson's murder.

Lawrence had a strong antipathy toward Rose, she told Morgan. Rose had started fist fights with her several times, threw knives at her once, rammed Lawrence's car with hers, and threatened her many times, probably because she saw Lawrence as a threat to her hold on Manthie.

This raised the question why Manthie would stay with Rose if she were such a dangerous person. The explanation, Lawrence said, was the daughter Valery: If anything happened to Manthie, Rose would have custody of the child, a prospect Manthie dreaded, although it's difficult to know whether he had genuine feelings of tenderness for the child or if he just wanted to stymie Rose. As a footnote to the interview, Lawrence mentioned that when she lived down the street from Manthie in Bremerton, her house was burglarized. She was certain the burglar was Rose.

The next morning after his talk with Jeanne Lawrence, Morgan took the unusual step of bringing Manthie downstairs from the jail to his office for a talk, reminding him that his lawyer wouldn't approve. Manthie didn't care what his lawyer said; he was just happy to be out of the jail for a while. It wasn't clear to Morgan whether Manthie thought this conversation would make him look as if he had nothing to hide or if he were simply naïve about what a subtle investigator might be able to trick out of him.

Did Rose burglarize Lawrence's house, Morgan asked. Yes, Manthie had seen some furniture at Rose's house and thought it was stolen.

Why didn't Manthie leave Rose if he was as close to Lawrence as he claimed? Because his family didn't approve of Lawrence, Manthie explained, an answer suggesting Lawrence wasn't as skilled as Rose at making first impressions.

Then Manthie posed a question to Morgan: Do you think I'm capable of murder? Morgan cut him off, explained that he didn't bring him from jail to talk about Edmondson's death. But Manthie continued with that topic and Morgan cut him off again, adding, "I don't believe you're innocent," then mentioned some of what he'd found that made him believe Manthie was guilty. But he wouldn't go further on the topic. After talking for about two hours, Manthie said he'd like to talk again. "All you have to do is ask," Morgan said.

In a further conversation with Mayselle Davis, Rose's neighbor on Long Lake Road, Morgan learned that Rose had wanted to talk with her about signing a cashier's check for $900. Rose had borrowed $800 from Davis, ostensibly to bail Manthie out of jail, but Davis didn't think Rose would go through with it because her attorney told her to leave him where he was.

So Morgan talked next with Chuck Arnold of Arnold's Bail Bonds and learned that yes, Rose had written a $500 check as a retainer on springing Manthie loose. Since then Rose talked to Arnold numerous times to check on the progress with the bail application, and once they had breakfast together. With Arnold's 10-year-old son present, and in a 10-minute conversation that puzzled Arnold, Rose repeated the story that her late husband was a homosexual, that he and his roommate Mike Cogswell used drugs and wanted Rose to get involved with them in kinky sex, and that Cogswell was the one who shot Edmondson.

* * *

Of continuing interest to the detectives was the fresh paint job inside the Gremlin—was it done before or after Edmondson's disappearance on the night of December 21? The former owner of the car reported that it had no fresh paint on the inside door panels when he sold it to Rose. Employees at Bob's Automotive in Bremerton had worked on the car off and on for several months – there was always something wrong with it, they said – but they couldn't be certain about when they noticed the new paint job on the inside, only that it looked like it had been done by an amateur.

On March 10, more than two months after the investigation began, the detectives received the report from the state crime lab on the items taken from the investigations of the Gremlin and Rose's house. Of pertinent interest: glass fragments found in the soles of Bill Edmondson's Pro Keds running shoes matched those taken from the floor of Rose's house; of the two hairs from the transmission hump of the

Gremlin, one was "microscopically similar" to Edmondson's head hair and "could have come from that source;" all 10 hairs analyzed had droplets of black spray paint adhering to them, suggesting that the black paint had been sprayed relatively recently; and the cast of the boot print found at the scene matched the size and sole/heel style of the boots Manthie wore.

On the other hand, photos of the tire tracks found near Edmondson's body didn't match the tread on the Gremlin, and the seven $100 bills taken from Manthie in his arrest by Port Orchard police yielded no useful fingerprints.

By mid March, while being prepped by prosecutors for her testimony in Manthie's upcoming trial, Mayselle Davis admitted that she'd been holding back some information because of her friendship with Rose. On the morning of December 22, the day Bill Edmondson failed to show up for work, she noticed something unusual at Rose's house next door—thick, black smoke was rising from the chimney. Manthie's explanation was that he was just burning some oily rags. That same morning, Davis said, Rose scrubbed the inside of the Gremlin with soap, and Ken, her husband, said he knew the person who had gotten Rose into the country with a fiancé visa in 1977, a man named Thorpe. This was undoubtedly the James Thorpe who signed her marriage visa application and stood her up when she arrived in Seattle. (On an INS document, a suspicious officer had written, "Was K-visa a ruse for her to enter US?")

Ken Davis also said that somehow Manthie passed word to Rose from jail that she'd better start visiting him or he'd start telling his attorney what he knew about the murder. As jail records showed, Rose promptly began making visits.

Apparently feeling the burden of what she'd been concealing, May Davis told Morgan that Rose had made a few non-committal comments about the murder and claimed that Edmondson's blood was in the Gremlin because he had frequent nosebleeds and because once, in an argument, she'd hit him on the nose with a flashlight. In this conversation with Davis, Rose insinuated again that Edmondson and Mike Cogswell were homosexual drug-users and that Cogswell either set up the killing or did it himself. Davis commented how strange it was that she had never seen Rose cry over her husband's death, never show remorse.

A few days later, the neighbor May Davis called Morgan again, this time to tell him that she wanted to get rid of some items Rose had brought to her house for storage: a box containing about 100 cassettes, a camera, some paintings, jewelry for a man, and other belongings. Cogswell later identified all the items as his and said he planned to press charges for theft.

Another search of Rose's house, this one on March 22, yielded two cans of black spray paint. The next day, Cogswell mailed Morgan an itemized list of things he said Rose had stolen from him, items that had been in the house he shared with the Edmondsons on This-A-Way: Furniture, clothing, a waterbed, lamps, rugs, and numerous other household items, 150 cassette tapes, and hundreds of copies of a magazine collection including *Penthouses*, *Playhouses*, *Que*, *Time* and *Newsweek*, to which Cogswell gave a total estimated value of $3,246. Even though a waterbed was one of the new items detectives noted on their search of Rose's house on March 23, Rose denied having any of these things.

While in jail awaiting trial, Richard Manthie proved that he'd failed to learn a vital lesson about incarceration. From his time in the state prison in Montana, he should have known that prisons and jails are inhabited by people like him, people eager for useful information, incriminating information about fellow inmates that they can trade with prosecutors in exchange for shortened sentences or other benefits.

One of these fellow inmates, a man named Fred Stocker, about to begin a five-year prison sentence for attempted rape, told the following story to Detective Morgan in the presence of his attorney and Chris Casad, the deputy prosecutor who would try the case against Manthie: In late March, Stocker said, he walked into Manthie's cell while Manthie was talking to another inmate, Jesse Noble, a sex offender awaiting sentencing.

According to Stocker, Manthie told Noble that he shot his ex-wife's husband twice in the head. Because Manthie denied this before, Stocker interrupted Manthie to ask him what he'd just said, and Manthie replied, "I shot the son of a bitch twice in the head and he still wouldn't die so I shot him again." Then, according to Stocker, Manthie said he put Edmondson's face in the mud and next day cleaned up the car.

The next day, Stocker said, Manthie denied the story and claimed he was just saying what the *prosecutor claimed* he had done, not what Manthie actually did, but Stocker didn't believe him and told him so, and Manthie didn't persist in his denial.

As the conversation ended, Stocker produced a note from Manthie, a note that Manthie gave to Noble and that Noble passed on to Stocker:

Nobel,

There is dollars on you ass – don't help pigs. Tham only crosse you.

its not two late, are them paying you two

someone can sent you dollars two. Cool

just you be cool dollars will get two you ok.

No one no this but you I Rick has nothing two do with this note.

Be cool man, thro this note in tolet.

The handwriting was disguised but the note was obviously Manthie's, an inducement for Noble to remain silent and a clumsy effort to deflect suspicion from himself.

The detectives were passed another note, this one plainly from Manthie:

*Jesse is Fred [Stocker] against me or what The way it looks in a way that he is the only two of you have I talked to with that kid listening at times but whats going on and Jesse answer this note tonight [*unintelligible*] Fred is not against me give him this note ok This envelope was closed when I sent it to you and why do they take him out [*unintelligible*] answer this note tonight and what did they asked and you what did you say [*unintelligible*] Fred send These notes back with you so [*unintelligible*] I no they wont go no where else*

When examined, both notes were found to bear Manthie's fingerprints.

By this time, Rose could well have been wondering what her ex husband might be saying to detectives or prosecutors about the murder to work a deal. But on April 2, she suddenly had something else to worry about. She was arrested that day and jailed on three charges of theft: Stealing money (a misdemeanor) from former boyfriend Jerry Dike, a sailor at Bangor in August, 1981; stealing $900 from another sailor who stayed the night at her house, a felony, in October 1981; and stealing personal belongings, a felony, from Michael Cogswell in

January or February 1982. Vincent and Marietta Barios, the Filipino immigrants who rescued Rose on her arrival in this country in 1977 and brought her to Bremerton, paid the $7,000 bail.

On April 8, Detective Magerstaedt had an unusual phone conversation with a 61-year-old man named Jett who reported that in late December he was leaving a restaurant in Silverdale when he saw two women standing next to a phone booth. As he was getting into his car, one of them approached him and asked for a ride to the Bangor Submarine Base. To make small talk along the way, he asked if her husband worked there, to which she replied, "Yes, the son-of-a-bitch blew his brains out yesterday." Jett described his hitchhiker as about 27 or 28 with long black hair and a dark complexion, but he wasn't sure if she were Filipino or Caucasian. He was sure that it was just before Christmas.

While doing a routine search of Manthie's cell on May 10, two jail officers came upon an envelope from a Wesley "Buck" Walker with a return address of Lompoc, California, the location of a federal prison. Walker's stay in the Kitsap jail overlapped with Manthie's. The officers' report of the discovery of the letter hinted at no recognition of Walker's name, even though in a broadly publicized case he was a marijuana grower from Hawaii who was convicted of the murder of a wealthy American couple on their sailboat on a remote island in the Pacific. He was the central figure in a book by Vincent Bugliosi and Bruce C. Henderson, "And the Sea Will Tell." Manthie was a pen pal of a celebrity killer.

By this time Manthie and the general public must have been wondering why it was taking so long for Rose to be arrested. The reason, prosecutors explained, was that while they had strong physical evidence against Manthie, they didn't have enough yet to arrest Rose, even though a recent ruling from the appeals court would allow them to use against her the statements Manthie made to Noble. In addition, they had little fear of her fleeing: She was too eager to get her hands on the $150,000 insurance money she believed she would she would get following Edmondson's death.

During his stay in the Kitsap County jail, Manthie made a noteworthy phone call to Rose at her Long Lake Road home. But it wasn't Rose who answered the phone. It was a man. Whatever Manthie believed until then about his relationship with her, he was quick enough at that moment to understand she'd already moved on, that he'd served his purpose for her and was now disposable, and that his only use to her now would be to give her cover – if he were willing, given this discovery. But, he might have wondered, why should I?

In May, the court ordered Manthie to provide a handwriting sample that they might match with the note to Jesse Noble, so on the 17th a detective and a woman from the prosecutor's office went to Manthie's cell. Manthie said he wouldn't talk without his attorney. After a phone call with his attorney, Manthie said he would comply. He began writing left-handed, which was obviously laborious for him, so the detective called the prosecutor and learned that Manthie was right-handed. The detective told Manthie to write with his right hand, but Manthie said he'd write however he wanted. After another five-minute call to Rainey, one of Manthie's attorney's, Manthie handed the phone to the detective; Rainey had instructed him to write as the detective told him to. So Manthie began writing with his right hand, but he guided it with the left, shaking it so that after seven or eight words, nothing was legible. After two hours they finally gave up.

Detective Morgan, though, had a productive day. A neighbor and friend of Pete Dugeno called him to report that when he went to the house with the coroner immediately after Dugeno's body was found, he saw a .12 gauge shotgun, a 300 Savage rifle, and what he thought was a .22 High Standard Derringer, and that these weapons came into Rose's possession on Dugeno's death.

In a longer phone conversation that same day with Mark Johnson in Albuquerque, Morgan learned that Johnson lived with Rose for a while on Long Lake Road and that he was serious about her until he learned some things he didn't like. Even though she inherited the house from Robert Erickson, she lied when she told him it belonged to her mother-in-law and that she had to charge him $200 per month in rent.

Johnson said he'd never met Richard Manthie, that Rose told him her former husband was a very dangerous man and that Johnson shouldn't make any trouble with him.

Starting in summer of 1981, Edmondson started coming to the house, Johnson said, and that he seemed like a very straight, simple guy. But Rose didn't want him around, he said, and urged Johnson to put him off, which Johnson did, telling him to get out.

Morgan continued pursuing the matter of guns. Johnson said Rose kept a .22 revolver between the mattress and the box springs and took it out once to wave it playfully at him and warn him what she's do if she caught him with another woman. He also said he thought she had a "Derringer-type pistol" and that there was a lot of ammunition around the house for both a .22 and a shotgun.

Before the phone interview ended, Johnson told Morgan a story about a trip he and Rose took to Portland, Oregon, and how on the way back they stopped for a night at a motel on the north side of the Columbia River in Vancouver, Washington. They got into a fight in the motel, with Rose screaming and clawing at him, and he slapped her. She left the room, got into the car, and reminded him that she had a gun and that she knew what to do with it. Johnson called the police but when they caught up with Rose and checked the car, they found no gun. Johnson however was charged with disorderly conduct. Finally he suggested that for more information about Rose, Morgan contact another of her former boyfriends, a man named Steve Stavnicki.

Next on Morgan's interview list was Joyce Elton, the older woman who worked with Rose at the hospital, who drove Rose to Edmondson's funeral in Pennsylvania, and who now volunteered for an interview with Morgan. Elton, a grandmotherly figure with light brown hair, was probably the most loyal friend Rose ever had. Elton told Morgan she'd known Rose for about three years, that she treated Rose like a daughter, and that they had grown very close. Although Elton has since died, to this day Rose still refers to her as "Mom."

Elton had lent money to Rose to pay the "rent" on the house Rose inherited debt-free from Erickson – remember that she was also collecting "rent" money from Mark Johnson – and she gave her a loan of $475 to buy the 1973 red and white Gremlin that was now in the sheriff's custody and being carefully examined inside and out. But her generosity and friendship had limits. No, she said, she did not give Rose a $2,000 loan for a down payment on the house she bought with Edmondson, as Rose claimed to detectives. That was a lie, she said, and despite their closeness, she would not lie for Rose. So the source of the down payment on the new house was still a mystery.

Elton told of taking Rose on a vacation to Reno and paying her way because she enjoyed Rose's company, and of accompanying Rose on the trip east for Edmondson's funeral in Pennsylvania, just to see that part of the country and to support her daughter-like friend. When the two of them looked at Edmondson's body in the casket, Elton felt there was something unusual about his hands, something that didn't look right. She thought about this for a time, and on the long drive back to Kitsap County, she asked Rose if Edmondson had been wearing his wedding rings when they saw him in the casket. No, Rose said with certainty, he wasn't. After riding a while longer, Elton realized what she thought was odd about Edmondson's hands: He was wearing his Navy white dress gloves. She asked Rose how she could be certain that he wasn't wearing his rings. "Oh, well," Rose answered quickly, "if they were going to put his rings on, they'd be on the outside of the gloves." Elton was puzzled that Rose would concoct something like this.

Were there other things she lied about? Morgan asked. Well, yes, when Elton learned that Manthie was in prison in Montana, Rose lied about it. No, she said, he wasn't. But when Elton learned from the newspaper that Manthie *was* in prison, she confronted Rose, who said he wasn't in prison; he was just in jail. Elton knew the difference but didn't know why Rose would lie about it.

Elton mentioned that at some time – she couldn't pinpoint the date – Rose and Richard showed up at her door and asked for money for an abortion. They couldn't afford another child, they explained, and Rose said she'd pay back the money. Given Rose's previous lies, a more skeptical, less trusting person would have wanted some proof of this alleged pregnancy, but Elton didn't. She gave Rose the money.

Morgan finally contacted 36-year-old Steve Stavnicki who, it turned out, was still in the County Sheriff's office in the Work Release Program. He admitted having been friendly with Rose and told about the night she had taken him out for dinner and a few drinks, after which they spent the night at her house on Long Lake Road, about discovering the next morning that $900 was missing from his pants pocket, and about Rose denying any knowledge of the money. As he told Morgan, he was already in trouble with the law on some other matter and didn't want to push this one. He also admitted feeling too foolish about the incident to report it to the police.

By this time the detectives were developing a portrait of Rose as an aggressively lusty young woman with only a casual relationship with the truth, a close relationship with alcohol, and a yearning for other people's possessions. Which is not to say she had no respect for property. As G.K. Chesterton said, "Thieves respect property. They merely wish the property to become their property that they may more perfectly respect it."

Over coffee one morning at a Denny's restaurant in Bremerton, Joyce Elton and three other hospital employees met for coffee to talk about Rose. They felt sorry for her at first, they said, because, she had a one-year-old child and her husband, Manthie, was in prison so they befriended this pretty, slender young mother with long black hair to her waist. She was a good worker at first, starting as a dishwasher, then a food server, then a cashier. She was kind and thoughtful to customers, especially old people, making conversation and helping them with their trays.

But once, she got in a fight with another employee, a Filipino woman, squirting her in the face with a hose, and security was called to break them apart. The other employee quit the job rather than work anymore with Rose.

The conversation turned to fellow employee Robert Erickson, Elton believing that with her husband in prison, Rose told Erickson she would divorce Manthie and marry the lonely Erickson if he would write her into his will.

These women said they'd go out with Rose to the bars at night, but Rose would soon leave her friends to sit with a table full of men. One night when she went out with Joyce, she picked up a man who took both women to his house in a remote part of the county where Rose went to bed with him, leaving Elton alone in the living room. "I was so mad and embarrassed," Elton said, "I never went out with her again." The other women told similar stories: It became embarrassing to be around her in bars, and after a time she came to work at the hospital smelling of alcohol.

One of these co-workers told of going with Rose to the enlisted men's club at the shipyard where Rose was turned away because she'd been getting sailors drunk and stealing their money. The Shore Patrol hauled her away for interrogating, dropping her friend off at the main gate where she had to find her own way home.

As the women continued their coffee, they told yet another version of Rose's arrival in this country. Contrary to other stories, they said the alleged fiancé Thorpe *did* meet her at the airport and that he took her to his apartment at Ft. Lewis, the army post south of Tacoma, but that when he came home one day he found her with a bunch of other soldiers so he kicked her out. These women could not have heard this version from anyone but Rose, and given Rose's casual relationship with the truth, it's impossible to know what really happened.

When the former co-workers talked about Jeanne Lawrence, Manthie's attractive, one-time girlfriend, they said that when Rose discovered she had a rival for Manthie's attention, she grabbed Lawrence by the hair and beat her head against the pavement until Manthie leaped over a porch rail and broke up the fight by smacking Rose on the head.

Somehow they also seemed to know about the parentage of one of the two daughters Rose left

114

behind in the Philippines, the daughters Rose said were the child of sailor Keith Ryan. No, Elton said, this girl was born just seven months after Rose met Ryan. She'd seen pictures of the girl, who looked Filipino, and said the father was the son of Rose's Filipino landlord.

So far, Rose was still free to continue her predations, and the detectives continued to gather evidence, but so far they didn't have enough to charge her with murder.

SIX

Richard Manthie's Trial

May 19—June 9, 1982

Manthie's trial began on a cloudy day with a 99 percent chance of rain, a not unusual day for Western Washington in May. If you looked across Sinclair Inlet from the front steps of the Kitsap County Courthouse toward the shipyard, you saw nothing but gray, the sky and the water the same color, both crowding in on you.

Before being selected for the jury, a Bremerton citizen was brought into a room in the courthouse to answer questions during *voir dire*. Besides the opposing attorneys, another man was there, a man the prospective juror had never seen and who wasn't introduced. "He had wolf eyes that looked right through you," the prospective juror said. "It made the hair on the back of my neck stand up. That's never happened to me before." His words were almost identical to ones used earlier by a female jail employee. The man sitting across the table from him was the defendant Richard Wayne Manthie.

But later, dressed for trial, Manthie looked very different from the man who was arraigned January 15 in a prison jumpsuit with his hands cuffed behind his back. He had tousled brown hair then, a faint moustache, and a short curly beard along the jaw line. Today, having been rigged up for facing a jury, he was clean-shaven and had a $25 haircut paid for by the citizens of Kitsap County. Transfigured into a young executive in a dark, three-piece suit with a white shirt, striped tie, and shiny shoes, he looked more like a young vice president striding confidently into a boardroom than a violent, habitual felon facing a charge of aggravated first-degree murder. A clothier might even have described his appearance as "sharp."

The presiding judge was 48-year-old Leonard Kruse, a large, patient man who spoke slowly in a deep voice. A Minnesotan, he was accepted at the highly competitive Carleton College in Northfield where, as a junior, he and a friend took the Law School Aptitude Test on a lark, even though he planned to go into medicine. The two made a bet: Whoever scored higher was the winner. Kruse won, scoring in the top tenth of the top one percent of all those in the country who took the test.

So, in an abrupt course correction, he went to the University of Washington Law School, worked for a while for the State Attorney General, then came to Kitsap County to work with the County Prosecutor, a man who had been a year ahead of him in law school. In January 1982, just in time for the Manthie trial, he was appointed to fill a vacancy in Superior Court. He had defended five or six murder cases, but this was his first major trial as a judge.

In a blow to the defense, he rejected a motion that funeral home photographs of Edmondson's body be excluded as evidence; they're too gruesome and sure to be prejudicial, the defense argued. Judge Kruse also rejected a defense motion to exclude photos of the boot print found near the body.

Next, the defense argued that the case be dismissed because Edmondson's body was released for burial or cremation, an act that constituted destruction of evidence and thus was a violation of Manthie's due process. At the same hearing, they moved to suppress all evidence gathered from the house on Long Lake Road, from Manthie himself, and from any vehicles he owned or operated. Judge Kruse rejected both motions.

Manthie was defended by Ron Ness, a Port Orchard attorney who graduated from Montana State law school and specialized in criminal defense. A large, laid back man with black hair and a monotone voice, Ness is an athletic man known by his handball opponents as a skilled player and respected by judges as an excellent trial attorney.

Ness was assisted by Roy Rainey, 27, another local attorney who had prosecuted misdemeanor cases in municipal court and defended in felony cases but had not yet prosecuted a murder case. Ness requested his assistance though because they had worked together before. Ness would take the lead, design the trial strategy and pick their witnesses.

The state was represented by Deputy Prosecutors Warren Sharpe and Christian Casad. Chris Casad was a large, outgoing, friendly, balding man with a roundish face and a developing paunch.

He liked a good joke, and detectives liked him because he did whatever he could to help them build a case. This was Casad's first case after recovering from a car accident that few people thought he would survive. He enjoyed going out with detectives after work for drinks, and after one of these sessions he went off the road and crashed into a building.

Sharpe, described as a "geeky" man who waddled a little and frequently pushed his glasses up on his nose, was considered a brilliant and meticulous prosecutor who customarily went far beyond what was expected of him. If asked to produce 10 pages of information, he'd produce 20 or 30. His desk was piled high with files. More were stacked on the floor.

Sharpe summarized the state's case for the jury of six men and six women. On the night of December 21, 1981, he said, after an evening of drinking, when Rose knew Edmondson was sufficiently drunk and could reasonably assume Manthie would be too, she drove her husband to her house on Long Lake Road, where the two men would collide.

As Sharpe told it, Manthie, quick to violence when drunk, was suddenly face to face with the man who had taken his place in Rosalina's bed. He tried to goad Edmondson into a fight, offering him a knife. Given his level of intoxication, Edmondson was barely able to stand, let alone fight, let alone understand what was happening. When he failed to respond, Manthie smashed him in the face with his fist. With blood flowing from Edmondson's nose,

Manthie suddenly feigned compassion and insisted on taking Edmondson to the hospital.

Sharpe summarized the story Manthie told his cellmates, who then passed it on to prosecutors: Once Manthie and Edmondson were in the Gremlin, with Edmondson in the passenger seat, Manthie, drunk but still able to operate the car, told Edmondson to roll down his window so they'd have some fresh air. Then he added, "Turn on the radio. A man should have some music when he dies." At that point he pulled out a .22 pistol and fired twice into Edmondson's left temple. Edmondson slumped forward but kept gurgling so Manthie drove back to the house to get help from Rose.

Climbing into the car and sitting behind the passenger seat, Rose held Edmondson up so he'd look like a regular passenger while Manthie drove to find a place in rural Kitsap County to dump the body. When they reached the tree farm off Lake Flora Road, Rose held up the chain blocking the entrance so Manthie could drive on through.

Sharpe described how they dumped the body face down in a puddle and, with Edmondson still gurgling, Manthie shot him twice more in the back of the head. They rolled him over and Manthie stomped on his chest, caving in the chest and ribs and rupturing his spleen, then turned him again face down in the water and pulled his jeans down to expose the buttocks to suggest homosexual activity.

Sharpe told how Manthie returned to Rose's house and, the next morning, how they scrubbed the interior of the car and tried to cover the blood with spray paint. But, he added, Edmondson had an unusual blood type, stains of which were found in the car, as were hairs similar to Edmondson's, hairs bearing the black spray paint used to conceal evidence of the murder.

The motive, Sharpe explained, was the $150,000 life insurance policy Rose had persuaded Edmondson to buy, the proceeds from Edmondson's military insurance policy, and the This-A-Way house on which the newlyweds had just bought mortgage insurance.

Sharpe explained to the jury the charge of aggravated first-degree murder: A murder committed in conjunction with at least one other crime. In this case, Manthie expected to share in the proceeds of the $150,000 life insurance policy; he assaulted Edmondson before murdering him; and he stole $400 from his victim's pants pocket. The penalty for this charge was life without chance of parole, a guarantee that if convicted Manthie would die behind bars.

It was a hard case to defend, as Manthie's lawyer Roy Rainey said years later. His chief hope was to create doubt around some of the state's witnesses, starting with Jesse Noble, a jail mate of Manthie, a less than sterling figure. Noble was an alcoholic who had been convicted of car theft and burglary, and after being arrested for indecent liberties with a child, he was arrested, then released on bail. He jumped bail and fled to Indiana, then to Mississippi where he was tracked down by the bail bondsman and returned to jail in Kitsap County. But he agreed to testify for the prosecution on an agreement that he'd serve time not in a state prison but in a sexual psychopath program at Western State Hospital—an agreement Rainey hoped would undermine his value to the prosecution. Besides, Rainey believed, Noble's version of Manthie's jail cell description of the crime could hardly be called a confession by Manthie.

Then he turned the court's attention to Rose and traced her background in the Philippines—how she and Manthie met at the Subic Bay Naval Station on Luzon, her illegal entry to this country on a fiancé visa with the help of a man who was already married, her abbreviated marriage to the 76-year-old Pete Dugeno and her inheritance of his property; her marriage to Manthie, and her curious association with Robert Erickson and inheritance of his property. He told of her tempestuous marriage with Manthie, acknowledging his imprisonment in Montana; her relationships with numerous men, including Mark Johnson, and her marriage with Edmondson, which is when she began planning his murder with Manthie's help, even by urging his release from prison and giving financial help for his return to Kitsap.

It was a weak defense, certainly not a claim of his client's innocence, merely an effort to portray him as a hapless tool, easily employed to help Rose reach her financial goals. Rose was the real evil, Manthie's lawyers said.

Anyone expecting high drama in the trial was probably disappointed. As in most murder trials, detectives and crime scene experts told in lumbering detail about the evidence – the hairs and blood stains in the car, the shards of glass in Edmondson's shoes and jeans, which could have been accumulated only in Rose's house where the crime began to develop, Manthie's cowboy boots and the match to prints found at the tree farm near the victim's body. Prosecutors even brought in the passenger-side door from the Gremlin.

A pathologist repeated his grisly description of the damage done to Edmondson's body, which he thought at first must have come from a truck traveling at high speed. He said it would take at least a 180-pound man to cave in Edmondson's chest as it was and to break so many ribs, or a much lighter person jumping from a four-foot wall.

Mike Cogswell testified about the Edmondson's quarrelsome marriage, Rose's incessant complaints about not having enough money, the poisoning attempts with Tylenol, and why, at Edmondson's request, he moved in with the newlyweds as a bodyguard. He read the passages from Edmondson's journal about waking up in the bathtub, covered with blood, the phone cord wrapped around his neck and he testified that Edmondson never notified the police about the incident because he wanted to catch her in the act and be a hero. He also said that just before Edmondson was killed, he was about to make his mother and stepfather the beneficiaries of his life policies because he didn't want Rose to get anything.

Neighbor May Davis testified about the defendant and Rose cleaning up the Gremlin on the morning of December 22 and about the black smoke coming from the chimney, which the prosecutor claimed signaled the attempt to burn some of the victim's clothing to hide evidence.

The prosecution's chief witness was Jesse Noble, who related a more graphic, more detailed account of what Manthie told him in their jail cell, an account portraying Manthie differently from the casual, quiet man in the courtroom who smiled and joked with his guards and lawyers. Noble testified that not only did Manthie describe how he killed Edmondson but that he did it with unusual enthusiasm. "He gets highly excited when he talks about it," Noble said. "His eyes get real big ... he said he gets an orgasm off something like that. He likes scary movies where people are cut up ..." In his gray suit and white shirt, Manthie listened intently, but he showed no emotional reaction other than slumping in his chair and staring at the blank legal pad in front of him.

Noble said Manthie and Rose had been planning Edmondson's death for months, corroborating that she'd visited him in prison in Montana in 1981 to further the plans, and related that she'd made two unsuccessful attempts to kill

Edmondson earlier, then told Manthie he'd have to do it himself when he was released from prison.

Their first plan, Noble said, was to get Edmondson drunk, put him in a car, get the car to a road with a steep drop-off, and push it over the edge. But the best opportunity came when Rose engineered the confrontation between her past and present husbands at her house, ensuring first that both would be drunk, and knowing that when's he drunk Manthie is at his most vicious.

According to Noble, Manthie gave varying versions of the meeting, but the one Noble told from the witness stand went like this: Trying to incite a physical confrontation, Manthie gave Edmondson a knife with which to fight back, but Edmondson wouldn't take it and Manthie called him a "candy ass" and said he'd kill him. Manthie even put a gun on the table and told Edmondson to pick it up. Whether Edmondson picked it up isn't clear, but Manthie then "kicked Edmondson in the face and busted his nose all to hell" and told Rose to "get a towel 'cause I don't want the son of a bitch bleeding all over my house."

Edmondson told Rose she wasn't getting any of his insurance money. She called him a lying son of a bitch and said to Manthie, "Kill him or I will."

At this point Manthie had to finish the job: having just violated the conditions of his parole by committing an assault, he knew he'd go back to prison. The rest of Noble's testimony repeated what

Prosecutor Warren Sharpe summarized in his opening statement – the drive to the tree farm, the dumping of the body, and the further damage done to it there. After shooting Edmondson in the head, "Manthie rolled him over and jumped on his chest and kicked the hell out of him," Noble testified, adding, "Manthie didn't want anyone finding him and have him become a vegetable and Rose have to take care of him."

Noble testified that Manthie told him there was "a lot of blood and brain fluid" in the car and that's why they had to clean it up and paint part of the interior.

Defense lawyer Ron Ness sought to discredit Noble, suggesting that Noble was lying, that he'd made a deal to go to a psychiatric hospital rather than prison where, as a pedophile, his chances of survival were dim, that he'd used Manthie to make life better for himself. He also summarized Noble's long criminal record.

Fred Stocker, another jail inmate mentioned earlier, corroborated Noble's story.

Judge Kruse refused to admit evidence about the $500 found on Manthie when he was stopped by Port Orchard police and about Rose's changing her name from Edmondson to Manthie on the employment records at Harrison Hospital just before she took out the mortgage insurance on the house she and Edmondson bought together near Lake Symington.

On June third, the defense promised to introduce evidence from Wesley "Buck" Walker, Manthie's former jail mate, then in the Federal prison at Lompoc, California, for his murder of two people in the South Pacific and the theft of their sailboat.

Like Manthie, Walker began his criminal career in childhood when he was charged several times with joy riding and escaping twice from juvenile detention. At 16 he was arrested for grand auto theft ("I just hung out with the wrong people at an impressionable age," he explained.) These activities were followed with charges of robbery, two burglaries, and armed robbery, for which he was sentenced to five to life in San Quentin. (His defense: "The gun wasn't loaded.") He violated drug laws in Hawaii, used phony identification to get a passport in the name of Roy Allen, and at one point was committed to a mental hospital for the criminally insane. Like Jesse Noble, Walker wasn't the ideal witness.

One of Walker's chief accomplishments was to be the only prisoner ever to escape from the McNeil Island Federal Penitentiary in Puget Sound. When he was captured, he was placed temporarily in Kitsap County jail where he became friends with Manthie. But Walker could be useful to the defense by testifying that Noble confessed to him that the only chance he, Noble, had to stay out of prison was to commit perjury by lying about Manthie's version of killing Edmondson.

With Walker imprisoned in California, attorneys for both sides flew to Lompoc to take Walker's video testimony at a cost of $1,100, but when they returned they found that the audio portion of the interview was gone, so Judge Kruse instructed them to find lip readers who could transcribe Walker's video testimony. Two lip readers watched the testimony but reported that Walker had what they called a "lazy mouth," so they couldn't recognize his words. Rather than agree to another trip to California, the judge agreed to take Walker's deposition by phone, to be played in court along with the videotape. If trial watchers were expecting something dramatic, they were disappointed to hear nothing of importance.

A handwriting expert identified Manthie as the author of the note to Noble, and prosecutors introduced another note from Manthie to another inmate, Jay Schoor:

Jay, look I don't want to see you go to prison but maybe you can work with this. I wil have my lawyer talk to you on what was said in tank 3 when you was with me there. First of all say that Noble asked you to back him up if he made a deal with the prosecuting attorney and that you could do the same thing. That is all you to no was to say that you heard me and him talking and that I said I had done it but you told him no for it was not true and you wanted no part of it and that at no time did ever said anything like that. Maybe you can make a deal on him lying about my case.

The note wasn't read in open court but was given to the jury later.

For followers of the case, one of the most anticipated days of the trial was Thursday, May 27, the day Rose was scheduled to testify. To shield her from questioning, her attorney had asked the court to quash the subpoenas from both the prosecution and the defense, but Judge Kruse refused to do it.

Over the preceding five months, almost every news story in the Pacific Northwest had linked her name with Edmondson's murder. She'd been portrayed as a Black Widow, had been investigated for other crimes, had been arrested for still others, and was always in the background during testimony at Manthie's trial as the driving force in her husband's death. Given the brutality of the murder and accompanying publicity, she was the kind of figure who attracted the attention of John Henry Browne, the Seattle lawyer with a keen nose for sensational cases. They have included the recent case of Colton Harris-Moore, the teenaged "barefoot bandit" who was convicted of a long series of break-ins in the Northwest as well as the theft of an airplane, a boat, and two cars; and the recent case of Robert Bales, the American soldier charged with slaughtering 16 civilians in Afghanistan in 2012.

Brown has been called a "walking ego." Tall, with long, swept-back hair and a well-developed skill of calling attention to himself, he entered the Kitsap

County courtroom with the diminutive Rose on his arm. She was garbed in innocence: A demure, wine colored, pleated dress with a Peter Pan collar decorated with cream colored lace and a tiny ribbon bow. High, wedge-heeled shoes made the tiny woman appear taller than five feet, one inch. The courtroom was full but conspicuously devoid of Filipinos, whose status in the community she'd shamed by her tawdry behavior. Judge Kruse banned cameras from the courtroom, and to minimize the hubbub, he allowed Rose to enter through the law library and the judge's chamber.

In response to questions by Ron Ness, she gave very few answers. She acknowledged that she was 28, that she came to this country in 1977, and that she had three children (two were still in the Philippines), that she'd been married to Agapito "Pete" Dugeno, Richard Manthie, and William Edmondson, but to every other question – How did you come to America? Do you know Ken and May Davis? Were you with your husband the night of December 21? She shielded herself with the Fifth Amendment, sometimes glancing to her attorneys for guidance. She answered no questions posed by the prosecutors. After about five minutes of essentially non-testimony, Rose left with Brown in his Mercedes.

When she came to the courtroom again, this time at the request of another lawyer who was representing her on some civil matters, she wore blue jeans, blouse and sweater. A news photographer was lying in wait for her, so she darted into the women's

130

bathroom to escape, but the photographer followed her, and later she raced down a hallway with the photographer in pursuit. When Rose ran downstairs to the first floor of the courthouse and out the door to the parking lot, the photographer snapped a photo of her with her sweater pulled over her head.

When the court convened on June 4, the defense took the risk of calling Manthie to the witness stand to give his own version of events on the night of December 21: He was at the Davis home next door to Rose's where he and Ken and May Davis drank "about a case of beer" when Rose called him and told him to come home. "I brought out some pictures I found that day," he testified. "There were nude pictures of a lady and a guy and a bunch of pictures of men. I asked who they were and what she had been doing while I was in prison. I asked if she was running a whorehouse ..."

"Rose yelled, 'You ain't ever gonna change! You're already drinking and accusing me of things.' That's when she told me we wasn't married. She said she was married to some guy in the Navy and I looked at her and laughed. I said, 'Don't expect me to believe that because I never signed no papers.' Then she showed me the military identification papers."

It's difficult to understand how Manthie couldn't have known he was divorced, although maybe his failure to show up in court for the final divorce proceeding, and maybe Rose's visits while he was in the Montana prison allowed him to sustain the delusion.

Trying to absorb the sudden news that he was no longer married to Rose, he testified that he poured himself a glass of Everclear, or "moonshine" as he called it. "Then we got into it about her lying to my parole officer and how he could send me back to prison and she said she was divorcing this guy Edmondson. I told her I was going to take our daughter away and she threw a glass at me and I slapped her on the forehead and left."

His next move, he said was to "get in the car, get some beer, go park someplace and get plastered." He felt like a fool, he told Ness, that he'd been lied to again, and now he'd have to go back to prison for the assault on Rose. He lost control of the car and went into a ditch, he said, so he went back to the house but Rose had locked him out so he broke the door in. Rose wasn't there so he sat on the couch, waiting for Rose to call the law on him, then went to bed.

He testified that the next time he saw Rose was the following morning when she was cleaning the Gremlin. He spent most of the day next door drinking with May Davis.

When Ness asked him about Noble's testimony, Manthie said he wasn't confessing to the murder, just summarizing the evidence prosecutors had against him. He was innocent, he said, but that Noble twisted the story and passed it on to a jailer,

132

who passed it on to Noble's lawyer, who used it to bargain a deal for his client.

The defense probably felt it had no choice but to have their client testify, but when Prosecutor Warren Sharpe began his cross-examination, the risk became clear quickly. Sharpe first challenged Manthie's claim that he didn't know Rose had divorced him, reading from letters that suggested otherwise.

Manthie acknowledged that under the terms of his parole from Montana, he wasn't to drink alcohol or go to places where alcohol is served, but he interpreted that to mean he was free to drink at home.

Did Manthie have any evidence that Rose had killed Pete Dugeno?

Objection.

Sustained.

Did Rose kill Robert Erickson?

Objection.

Sustained.

Did he help Rose spend any of the $12,000 she inherited from Dugeno?

No.

How did Edmondson's blood come to be in the Gremlin, and how did glass fragments from the floor of the house get into Edmondson's jeans and shoes?

He didn't know.

Had Manthie seen the police photos of the cable blocking the entrance to the dirt road where the victim's body was dumped?

Another nervous laugh, with a glance toward the judge in hopes of intervention. It didn't come.

No, he answered.

As the questions kept coming, Manthie's façade of composure slowly began to fade, and as the questions kept coming, his answers were interspersed with nervous laughs.

When the trial resumed after the weekend, Rose was there to testify for the defense. She wore a conservative black and beige two-piece suit, but her hair was untied and her face looked puffy, as if she'd been crying.

Were you ever married to Pete Dugeno?

Yes.

Did you know Robert Erickson?

She refused to answer.

Under her lawyer's questioning, she said she was living at her home on This-A-Way, although other testimony had her living on Long Lake Road and receiving her mail there.

When did you marry Bill Edmondson?

She refused to answer.

Were you with Bill Edmondson the night of December 21, 1981?

No answer.

What kind of car do you own?

No answer.

Who is the father of your three children?

She refused to answer.

In the few minutes this questioning took, Rose looked back and forth between her attorneys to know how to respond.

When testimony ended, Sharpe began his summation by drawing sympathy for young Edmondson "who had a right to have children and to live his life to its natural, fruitful conclusion." He reminded jurors of Noble's graphic testimony about Manthie's confession, of Rose's life insurance

policies from which Manthie would benefit, of
Noble's ability to describe the murder weapon and
his knowledge of the no-trespassing sign across the
entrance to the tree farm, even though the sign is
barely visible in police photographs of the scene, the
match between the glass in the victim's clothing and
the glass from the floor of the house. "It all fits," he
said.

In response, Ness pointed out that Manthie
was not named as a beneficiary of the policy on
Edmondson's life, that no proof had been offered that
Manthie took the rings or the money from
Edmondson's body, or that Manthie and

Edmondson had ever met, and that Noble and Stocker
were unreliable witnesses whose testimony had, in
effect, been bought by the prosecutors. Finally he
deflected attention from his client to Rose, the one
who would certainly benefit from the murder:
"Rosalina Edmondson. You don't see her here today,
but she will have her day in court."

When the jury got the case that afternoon,
Tuesday, June 9, Judge Kruse gave them four
options: They could find him not guilty, guilty of
aggravated first degree murder, guilty of first degree
murder, or of second degree murder. They had 15
days of testimony to consider and almost 200 pieces
of evidence.

They found him guilty the next day, which
wasn't a great surprise to most people, and while the
jurors agreed not to talk to reporters, both the

prosecutors and the defense said the testimony of Noble and Stocker carried the most weight. The jurors also found the assaults on both Edmondson and Rose to be aggravating factors, which pointed to life without parole.

Little effort was put into a pre-sentence investigation, his sentence having already been determined by statute. Much of the document repeats what was written in Montana before his imprisonment there: He was reportedly run over by a rotor tiller when he was two, causing head injuries, a mild concussion, and a speech difficulty calling for therapy while in school. There was the possibility of some brain damage, but not enough to affect his behavior.

The psychological evaluation in Montana portrayed him as having average intelligence, feelings of inadequacy, and emotional instability. He was described as rigid, lacking insight, retaliatory, and suspicious, with an antisocial personality and borderline psychotic tendencies. The report said he needed structure and accountability, something Manthie himself might have intuited earlier when he enlisted in the Marines. Asked about his long-term goals when he was released, he expressed interest in auto mechanics and counseling delinquent youth, preferably small children.

In his brief pre-sentence interview with a Probation and Parole Officer in Kitsap County, he expressed hostility toward his punishment; he'd "gotten the shaft," he said. "A quick shuffle." He demanded attention but refused to cooperate when it was offered to him, and he denied all involvement in the criminal activity leading to his previous felony convictions. The interviewer, expressing incredulity at the judgment in Montana that he was a non-violent offender, concluded instead that he represented a tremendous risk to re-offend.

* * *

Many years later, reflecting on the case from his office, a new, white-walled space with light wood molding and an Ansel Adams photograph on the wall behind him, defense attorney Roy Rainey said he never asked Manthie if he pulled the trigger that put four bullets in Bill Edmondson's head. "You have to appear sincere about your position as his defender, so it's just easier not to know. There was a possibility Manthie might be found not guilty, but not much of one.

"That case was unique in terms of evidence," Rainey continued, "lots of hearsay and other inadmissible evidence that should have been objected to but wasn't. Judge Kruse could have excluded some of that evidence and seemed surprised that the attorneys on both sides failed to make objections when they could have, but both sides seemed to believe that Rose was the mastermind, and both sides needed that evidence to make their case against her."

Rainey perceived that Manthie was not very bright but thought he was, that he was brighter than the detectives. He even *wanted* to testify, Rainey said. "There was a lot of circumstantial evidence against him, and jurors would want an explanation from him about that. Besides, Noble's testimony almost necessitated that Manthie testify on his own behalf, as poorly prepared as he was to handle himself under cross-examination. On the other hand, if he had followed counsel's advice and not testified, he might have been able to appeal on the grounds of ineffective counsel."

He also failed to grasp the subtlety of the defense strategy, Rainey said. He claimed all along to be innocent, but his lawyers were trying to insinuate throughout the trial that he was Rose's tool. He didn't want to be seen as *anybody's* tool; to be seen that way would undermine his effort to appear innocent and make him guilty as an accomplice. So his own stubbornness might have helped ensure that he'd get the harshest sentence short of death.

At his sentencing, Manthie maintained his innocence and later filed an appeal on several grounds. He argued that photos of Edmondson's body at the tree farm and in his casket were designed to prejudice the jury and thus constituted prosecutorial misconduct. The court should not have allowed evidence of aggravating circumstances, he said. The court erred in allowing evidence not substantiated by the crime lab and other evidence that was "merely cumulative." It erred again, he claimed, by allowing Noble's testimony when his credibility was questionable.

The appeals court found no justification for overturning the verdict, so in 1981, at age 25, Richard Wayne Manthie had to start adjusting to the fact that he'd be in prison forever.

* * *

After Manthie was tried and convicted, and Rose hadn't even been arrested, he might have wondered if he alone were going to pay the price for Edmondson's death. During this period, her former hospital co-worker, Wes Niquette, noted her worsening condition. "Her personal hygiene deteriorated badly," he noted, "maybe because she was drinking a lot and under stress from the murder investigation. Her attendance got erratic; she phoned in sick a lot or just didn't show up."

For Christmas, she gave him a billfold with a dollar in it. He wondered if they had been stolen.

"She always wanted something from people and seemed to believe they owed her something. When I was trying to sell a piano, she offered me only half of what it was worth and thought I should just give it to her for that. When I sold her a portable TV, I had to pester her for three to four months before she paid me."

* * *

At this point, although out on $7,000 bail for the theft charges, Rose was still free to seduce and manipulate men as she'd done so successfully before, and she could look forward to the distribution of

Robert Erickson's estate, which could pay for her defense in the theft charges filed by Cogswell and others from whom she'd stolen money and other belongings. Meanwhile Manthie had to wonder about this: Could he surmount his attachment to Rose, implicate her in the murder, and testify against her at trial in hopes of a shorter sentence?

The authorities had several reasons for waiting to arrest Rose. While they had enough evidence to arrest Manthie – his boot prints found near the body, the blood in the house he shared with Rose, the broken glass found in the house and in Edmondson's shoes, the extent of the physical damage to Edmondson's body – they didn't have enough yet on Rose. Besides, they didn't consider her a flight risk; they knew her well enough to believe she'd stick around to collect the life insurance money she thought was her due. There was also hope that evidence allowed in Manthie's trial would strengthen their case against Rose.

Manthie didn't have to wonder much longer. Three days after his conviction, two sheriff's deputies went to her house with a warrant for her arrest for first-degree murder. After she was handcuffed, she asked to go inside to close down the fire and turn off the television. As she went to the couch to pick up her purse, one of the deputies prudently intervened and picked up the purse himself. They recited her rights, which she said she understood, then transported her to the Kitsap County jail.

A search of her house after her arrest yielded numerous items stolen from the hospital: A ham, some cheese, linens, scrubs, and silverware. Other stolen items were found at her house on This-A-Way.

"She tried to stay in contact with us at the hospital after her arrest," Niquette said, "but it was always 'do this, do that, bring me this'."

At her arraignment, Rose pled not guilty of her husband's murder. In lieu of $200,000 bail, she was held in custody.

SEVEN

Rosalina's Trial

February 16—March 5, 1983

Rose's trial for her husband's murder was scheduled for August 5, 1982, but soon after her arrest an interesting disclosure forced a delay: She was six months pregnant, she said. Marietta Barrios, the friend who welcomed her when she arrived in Bremerton, treated her like a daughter, bringing her maternity clothes and other necessities. But Rose complained to her and her husband that they weren't getting her a lawyer, and eventually they quit corresponding with her and accepting her phone calls. Again, she just wore out her friends.

The news of her pregnancy invited speculation about the identity of the father. If she was accurate about her due date, Manthie could be ruled out because he was in a Montana prison at the time of conception. Edmondson was still alive but seems like an unlikely candidate: Rose wasn't even living with him, and it isn't likely that she'd risk conceiving a child with the man she planned to murder. Finally, it's possible Edmondson was dead by the time the child was conceived.

The judge assigned to the case, 48-year old Robert Bryan, was a native Bremertonian, a graduate of the University of Washington School of Law, and a practicing attorney before being nominated a Kitsap

County Superior Court judge in 1967. Judge Bryan, about six foot three, an athlete in high school and college, was distinctive for reaching his position in Kitsap County's Superior Court at just 32. A dark haired man, he was always well dressed and well groomed. Furthermore, he wasn't aloof but made himself available to prosecutors and was always happy to explain his rulings. Mellow on the bench, he was a lawyer's judge, respected for his fair rulings. He became one of the finest judges in the state.

Concerned that the birth of the child might occur during the trial as it was first scheduled, Bryan agreed to delay the trial, a confusing strategy because Rose gave varying dates for the delivery. A judicial conference was another reason to delay. The date was reset to September 21.

In the pre-trial activities, Rose was represented by Roger Hunko, a Port Orchard attorney who specialized in high profile criminal cases. A body builder who ate continually and carried a small cooler filled with broccoli and cauliflower, he was like other criminal lawyers in that he was able to serve unlikeable clients by remembering his professional responsibility to defend them. Quiet, steady, pleasant, friendly, he smiled and laughed easily.

Rose couldn't afford the flamboyant John Henry Browne, so he disappeared from the picture, as did another Seattle defense lawyer named Allen Ressler. Rose's explanation for Browne's withdrawal was that she'd had an affair with him and that he withdrew when she ended it. It's more likely that both men chose not to represent a client whose stories weren't consistent and who likely wouldn't be able to pay them.

Because of the extensive publicity about the case before and during the trial of Richard Manthie, and the lingering intimations of Rose's involvement in the murder, Hunko moved for a change of venue and suggested that if Judge Bryan denied the motion, jurors should be brought in from another county.

The trial was postponed again when Hunko also withdrew, so Rose had to start over, this time with Seattle attorney Steve Moen, a graduate of the University of Washington and a 1966 graduate of the University of Michigan Law School. Moen was assisted by Dominic Santiago, a native Filipino who spoke Tagalog, Rose's native language. The new date was in mid October, after the child was born.

In the meantime, as a Navy widow Rose received free medical care at the Naval Regional Medical Center in Bremerton where her doctor planned to deliver the child by Caesarean section, the procedure to require a stay of five to seven days. An armed guard would have to be posted around the clock at a cost to the county of $300 to $350 a day, and a jail officer would have to accompany her on each of her hospital visits.

It's easy enough to believe that Rose was manipulating the system when she gave the court yet another due date – sometime between December 15 and January 15, 1983, although it's not clear why Rose was allowed to fix the date rather than her doctor.

During all this time, expenses were mounting for the jail. She had to have a cell by herself; she had to be transported to the hospital for her regular visits; and after a false labor she was driven by ambulance. And there would be the cost of busing jurors from neighboring Pierce County every day of the trial. Rosalina Edmondson was costing Kitsap County a great deal of money.

Finally, on January 6, 1983, at 8:30 AM at the Naval Regional Medical Center, Rose gave birth to a boy she named Shane Michael Edmondson. On the Certificate of Live Birth, no father is named. The infant was soon put in foster care and her trial was ready to begin. Judge Bryan ruled that no testimony would be allowed about Rose's history with Dugeno and Erickson, neither having a bearing on the case.

Much of the evidence presented to the jury by prosecutors Chris Casad and Warren Sharpe was presented earlier in Manthie's trial, especially physical evidence gathered from Rose's house and the Gremlin. Detectives Morgan and Magerstaedt testified, as did Mike Cogswell, who described his role in Edmondson's life as a "bodyguard," and John Niles, Edmondson's immediate supervisor at the submarine base, some of whose testimony paralleled Cogswell's.

May Davis added that in the morning after Edmondson's disappearance, Rose had come to her house to use the washing machine, something she'd never done before, and that the smoke billowing from Rose's chimney was black rather than the usual gray, suggesting that Rose was burning bloody clothes and washing away evidence. Davis also testified that when she got up in the morning she found a provocative note from Rose on her door: "Come over and see if I'm still alive."

Another witness was corrections officer Linda Pendleton, who'd been assigned to drive Rose to her medical appointments at the hospital and who reported this statement from Rose: "The only evidence the state would have against me is what Richard would say, and he wouldn't say anything." The defense was unhappy about this testimony but Pendleton insisted she hadn't solicited the comment from Rose, that Rose volunteered it herself, so Judge Bryan allowed it.

Crime scene investigator Doug Hudson reappeared to testify about physical evidence and gave what amounted to a primer on the difference between blood smears and blood spatterings and what kinds of information each provides. One smear on the passenger seat head rest in the Gremlin, for example, revealed that "probably a bloody head" brushed against the upper part of the passenger seat, while the spatterings above and in front of the right front door panel told him that the blood there had hit the surface at a high velocity and that it came from driver's side of the vehicle.

An expert from the state crime lab returned to explain once again the rarity of Edmondson's blood type and how the samples taken from the Gremlin couldn't possibly have come from either Rose or Manthie.

Jesse Noble returned to tell again the story Manthie told him with one added detail: When Manthie told about stomping on Edmondson's chest, "He said it sounded like a bag of potato chips breakin'."

Jurors also watched the video-taped deposition of Fred Stocker, which pretty much paralleled that of Jesse Noble. But he added that Manthie showed him a legal pad on which he'd listed seven points prosecutors had against him, explaining that he had answers for all of them. The seventh one on the list: "My wife won't talk."

Replying to Manthie, Stocker said, "If you're thinking of using those things as a rebuttal for your case, you better take the seventh one out of there, because if your wife wasn't involved, then there won't be anything for her to talk about, will there?" Stocker said he wasn't sure if that sank in or not.

Trying to mitigate the risk for his client, defense attorney Moen tried to get Judge Bryan to throw out the four factors that could result in an aggravated murder charge if Rose were convicted. He was only partially successful: The judge refused to throw out the prosecutors' claim that Rose solicited Manthie to commit the murder, so in effect the effort at amelioration failed. Short of a death penalty, she could get the stiffest penalty possible.

The prosecution called another witness, Allen Brown, Rose's co-worker at the hospital, who told of a conversation he'd had with Rose about the crime. They were talking about the house Rose inherited from Robert Erickson on Long Lake Road when Rose said, "Al, if you help me out on this, I'll give you the house." Recognizing it as a bribe, Brown declined the offer.

Rose's defense attorney, Steve Moen, who reserved his opening statement until late in the trial, told the court he could dispute little of the prosecutors' version of the murder but that he would dispute the conclusion they drew from it. He would challenge the credibility of key witness Jesse Noble; he admitted that Rose had had a lot of men in her life; he suggested that Manthie's jail cell "confession" came after he called Rose at home from jail, heard another man's voice on the phone, and was driven by rage to falsely implicate her in the crime.

When Rose finally took the witness stand, Moen elicited her story, including the details of all the men in her life from the time she left the Philippines until the night Edmondson disappeared. She admitted lying to Manthie's probation and parole officer in Port Orchard about still being married to Manthie because, she said, she wanted to hasten his release from prison so he could straighten out his life. "Because he promised me he gonna change his life" and help her remodel her house. At times, Moen had to pause while his client sobbed and wiped her eyes.

On her visits to see Manthie in prison, did she plot with him to murder Edmondson? No, she said.

She said it wasn't her idea to buy the life insurance policies but Edmondson's, and when telling of the last time she saw her husband, at the Sea Deck Restaurant on the night of December 21, she sobbed again.

She admitted she had concealed from Manthie her marriage to Edmondson but said that on the night of December 21st she told him and showed him her military ID. He punched her and she said, "You asshole, don't ever come back here because I'm going to turn you in to police. You assaulted me and I'm gonna send you back to prison."

When his turn came, Prosecutor Casad asked her accusingly about the statement Rose made to jail officer Linda Pendleton that Manthie wouldn't say anything to implicate her in the murder, and in an angry, teary outburst to the jury she acknowledged making the statement. "Yes, sir, because I didn't do anything. I didn't do any crime. I didn't hurt anybody." Moen having described the love-hate relationship between Manthie and Rose, Rose said many of her actions, including her visits with Manthie in the Kitsap jail, arose from her fear of him.

Casad continued to hammer at the inconsistencies between her testimony and the physical evidence in the case and got her to admit that she'd lied to detectives about her activities on the night of the murder. Sometimes shouting, she repeated that she feared that Manthie would hurt her or kill her.

Earlier testimony revealed that it was late on December 29, 1981, the day Edmondson's body was found, that sheriff's deputies told Rose about her husband's death, and that as early as the next day she went to a lawyer to collect on the life insurance. A representative from the insurance company said a letter from the lawyer dated December 31 showed a telltale sign: The date of Edmondson's death was said to be December 29, but it was clear that an alteration had been made – an earlier date, December 22, had been smudged out. The clear implication was that Rose knew about Edmondson's death a week before being told by the deputies that his body had been found. Rose denied knowing about the change in the letter, and when challenged about inconsistencies in her testimony, she said she lied out of fear of Manthie or was too confused and upset over her husband's death to remember details.

In his summation, Casad said, "The bottom line in this case, ladies and gentlemen, is that the defendant is more concerned about money, and the possibility of money, than she is about human life and the lives of her men."

In his instructions to the jury, the judge allowed only two choices besides acquittal: First-degree murder and aggravated first-degree murder. He ruled out murder in the second degree, the possibility that Rose became involved in the murder unexpectedly.

Rose wasn't in the courtroom for the reading of the verdict; earlier in the morning she collapsed in her cell. On hearing of the conviction, the judge, Moen and Casad went to the jail where Rose was face down in a padded cell. She was examined by a physician's assistant at the jail who said she seemed to be in some acute distress and was physically ill.

After almost three weeks of testimony from 55 witnesses, it took jurors no more than eight hours to find her guilty of aggravated first-degree murder. The aggravating circumstance was that she solicited Manthie to commit the murder and paid him or promised to pay him for doing it.

In a post-verdict interview at the courthouse, jurors said they tried to find something in Rose's favor, something to mitigate the most serious charge. "You don't know how we tried to find anything to help her out," one juror said. They just couldn't do it. "We believe she lied forwards, backwards, and upside down," said another. Many said her frequent sobs and protestations of innocence were a sham, not expressions of genuine feeling. "When you went over the testimony, it just seemed like she was able to turn it off and on and wouldn't conveniently answer certain questions," the foreman said. Another said she was moved at first by Rose's extravagant display of emotion. "But by the second day, I got completely used to it and it didn't mean a thing to me."

But the conviction wasn't the end of bad news for Rose that day. Less than 12 hours after hearing the verdict, she learned that her baby, a boy, placed since birth in a foster home, had just died of sudden infant death syndrome. On the line on the birth certificate identifying the child's father, we read "None Named." But in an undated letter requesting copies of the autopsy report and the certificates of the birth and death, Rose gave some evidence of the identify of the child's father by requesting that the grave marker read as follows:

Born January 6, 1983
Died March 5, 1983
Shane Michael Aldrich

If there were an Aldrich, he has not been identified.

After the trial, in an interview at the jail, Rose continued to play her game, insisting that money meant nothing to her. "I love my husband Bill, you know, not just for his money, you know. Money's nothing to me. I'm praying day and night to our dear Lord Almighty that I will get out of this mess because I'm not guilty. I never hurt anyone. Richard told me he's going to take me down to the river with him. And he did a good job."

She said the father of the just-buried child was Mark Johnson, the sailor who lived with her after Manthie was arrested for the murder and who was probably the man who answered the phone when Manthie called her from jail. Despite what Johnson said, Rose claimed that he still wants to marry her in spite of her conviction. "He sticks beside me."

At her sentencing Rose, was unrepentant and unbowed. "You're happy now, Mr. Casad?" she yelled. "You convicted an innocent people. You'll have my conviction on your conscience for the rest of your life."

She turned to those attending the sentencing hearing and thanked those who came to her son's funeral. She proclaimed her innocence again, and when Judge Bryan asked if she wanted to speak, she said, "I'm letting all people of this court know that I am not guilty. I will appeal for my rights. I am not guilty as long as I can talk."

The lawyer who handled her appeal, a faculty member at the University of Seattle School of Law, saw her case differently. He believed that Manthie was the instigator, not Rose. He acknowledged that she was involved in the clean up after the murder, which is what Rose insisted to me years later in one of our prison interviews: "No, I did not kill Bill. I just do what Richard tell me: 'Clean up the mess'."

The appeals attorney also believed there was some racism involved in her conviction: A prejudice based on the perception that Filipino women were loose-living. (It was a prejudice, but one Rose had done her best to enforce.)

But what he overlooked was all the planning Rose put into the murder, probably starting with her conning Edmondson in marriage by the false claim of

154

pregnancy, then continuing her efforts to gain Manthie's early release from prison, and her buying insurance on Edmondson's life. In Rose's mind, these activities have no connection to her husband's death.

Her appeal was based on five arguments: The trial judge allowed hearsay testimony; there was insufficient evidence to support the conviction; prosecutorial misconduct denied her a fair trial; the judge's instruction on first-degree murder was misleading; and although one of her lawyers spoke Tagalog, she claimed she was unfairly denied the use of an interpreter at trial. (During her trial, she asked for clarification of questions some 75 times but never asked for help from the interpreter who had been provided at the county's expense.)

As part of her appeal, she submitted a supplemental brief filled with statements that conflicted with other versions of her past or that shaded facts in her favor. She said she was unable to complete school because of the death of her parents, for example, and that at age 11, she was working as a seamstress in Manila, and that she "was introduced" to Keith Ryan, rather than saying how a prostitute usually picks up men. And she skipped over her marriage to the 76-year-old Pete Dugeno to get to her marriage with Manthie.

The appellate court rejected all her claims, dispensing with some of them in just two or three sentences. Thus did Rosalina Mendoza Dugeno Manthie Edmondson, like Richard Wayne Manthie, become what is known in the penal world as an L-WOP (life without parole) at the Women's Correctional Facility, Gig Harbor, Washington, where a sign on the highway nearby warns drivers not to pick up hitchhikers.

After three or four years of attempts to have her conviction overturned, Rose finally wore out the lawyer who handled her appeal, just as she eventually wore out her trial lawyer and her former supporters with her incessant demands for favors.

Her daughter Valery was sent to California to be raised by a distant relative and to get treatment by a therapist for the troubles she'd seen in her first five, turbulent years.

In what one might see as an illustration of cosmic justice, when Rose was charged in Bill Edmondson's death, she was offered the chance to accept the lesser plea of second degree murder. Rejecting legal advice, and still insisting on her innocence, she turned it down. If she hadn't, she probably would have been released by the early 1990s and be free today to carry on her predations.

EIGHT

Washington Corrections Center For Women, 2000

Except for the 12-foot chain link fence surrounding the complex, a fence topped with coiled barbed wire that glistens in the sunlight, the Washington Corrections Center for Women might be mistaken for a modern high school campus. Built in 1971, the 75-acre prison site sits atop a plateau surrounded by tall conifers near the town of Gig Harbor off State Highway 16.

Like all 858 prisoners there, when Rose arrived she went through a reception/admission/orientation process that certified she was legally committed and that included a thorough search of her body and her possessions, a shower and shampoo, and the issue of state clothing. She was photographed and fingerprinted, the birthmark on her thigh was noted, and she underwent a medical, dental, and mental health screening. She was assigned a Department of Corrections number and a specific housing unit according to the level of supervision she required at the time.

She went through an orientation process that informed her of the prison rules, the process for communicating with the prison staff, the Prison Rape Elimination Act and the reporting of sexual misconduct, the department's zero tolerance policy, and information on opportunities for education, work, recreation, religion services, and health care.

She was informed about self protection strategies, protection against retaliation, and behaviors that might be precursors to sexual misconduct, and she received instruction about the confidentiality ensured in cases of sexual misconduct, the availability of counseling and treatment, the requirement that staff report allegations, and the disciplinary actions that would result from making false allegations. And at that point, theoretically at least, she was ready for the rest of her life.

Unless she was considered dangerous, she would have access to adult basic education, an opportunity to earn a GED, take courses in technical design, information technology, and ornamental horticulture. She could take part in programs offered by Toastmasters, Alcoholics Anonymous, and Narcotics Anonymous. She could get chemical dependency counseling and take courses in creative writing, diversity awareness, HIV/AIDS, speech, theatrical movement, and meditation. All in all, she had more opportunities for self-improvement than she'd had since leaving school in the sixth grade. The only cost was her freedom.

* * *

By the time I learned about Rose and the basic elements of her story, she had been a prisoner for 17 years and, having in that time over-taxed and worn out her few friendships with her importunities – "Bring me new clothes." "Bring me some jewelry." "Bring me quarters for the vending machines." "Call my lawyer and tell him to get me out of here." – she had few visitors and was eager for a visit from a writer (a male writer) interested in telling her story.

At check-in, I stored my belt and the contents of my pockets in a locker as instructed, passed through a screener, and was told to wait on a bench along a corridor with other visitors until we were told to follow a female guard in a navy blue uniform. She led us outside, then through a series of locked, chain link doors and a small room until we arrived in what looked like a modern high school cafeteria where the tables and benches were fixed to the tile floor and vending machines waited at one end of the room. We visitors spread out at different tables and waited.

After a short time, prisoners streamed into the room and headed first for the vending machines to buy candy and chips and soft drinks, then joined their friends or family members at the tables. While I had photos of Rose, they were taken at least 17 years earlier and wouldn't necessarily portray her as she was that day. Still, none of those inmates in the room looked like a five foot, one inch Filipino. She knew I was coming, so I waited and watched the inmates, their visitors, and the hovering guards. There was nothing extraordinary about the appearance of the inmates. Dressed in civilian clothes, they might have been your daughter, your sister, or your child's Sunday school teacher. Most of the guards were beefy, dour looking women stuffed into too-tight uniforms.

I waited fruitlessly for half an hour, then left. A few days later Rose sent me a letter written on

lined notebook paper. She apologized for not
meeting me as scheduled, explaining that she'd been
in the hole and was dressed in an orange jump suit
and shackles, and didn't want to talk with me through
glass. She wanted to be able to talk with me face to
face and shake hands.

The hole, or "segregation" as prison
authorities call it, is 80 square feet, with a bed, toilet
and sink. Prisoners there are checked every 30
minutes and allowed out one hour in 24 for exercise.
All activities, meals and medications are recorded.
Rose, I learned, was in the hole frequently,
sometimes for weeks.

On my next visit, she was clothed in what I
guessed was her dressiest outfit—a turquoise and
ivory jogging suit, and plenty of lipstick. This was
clearly an occasion for her. She put her arm in mine
and escorted me to a wall decorated with a quilt with
a pattern of heart-shaped balloons where we posed
while another inmate took photos with a Polaroid
camera. In the margin of one she wrote, "To:
Robert—God Bless U always. Rose." On the other:
"To: Robert—Friends Forever—Rose." She
decorated the margins with numerous hearts.

She was 46 then, and while 17 years'
imprisonment had turned her pudgy, pasty-faced and
slack-breasted, it hadn't dimmed her habit of quick
physical contact with men or her excessive
friendliness on first meeting.

When we began our talk in the visiting room,
she told me about her background in the Philippines.
(She had told a different story to Manthie: That her

parents died in a jitney accident and that she grew up on the streets.) She talked about Ferdinand Marcos, the convent school, and the American sailors she met. Thanks to Marcos, "my dad," she called him, she said she had everything she needed when growing up, and after Rose's parents died, Marcos even bought Rose's grandmother a tavern so she could support herself and Rose. "My dad said it was a good idea for me to leave the Philippines because war was coming." (She was probably referring to the military efforts by the Muslim minority group, the Moro's, to gain their independence from the Christian majority government led by Marcos, who had by then become dictator.) "He helped me get my visa," she claimed.

She worked in the prison kitchen, she told me, for 42 cents an hour, the previous month earning about $30, but when she's in the hole for violating the rules, her income is less. "But I try to get along with everybody because prison authorities can make it very hard on you if you don't." Having seen some of the guards, I had no trouble believing her. She reads law books in the prison library, she claims, and she works on her case. In the cell she shares with another inmate, she has a small black and white TV. One of her prison friends was Mary Kay LeTourneau, the teacher and married mother of four children who'd had an affair with one of her elementary school students.

Valery, then 22, had come to visit recently, Rose said, and also visits her father and helps her parents communicate with one another.

Rose is resigned to being where she is, she implied, but moments later talked about her hopes of getting out, about Noble's testimony having been perjury, about trying to come up with money to hire a lawyer to fight on for her. Could Valery afford to hire a lawyer for her? Rose said she'd have to talk with her husband first. "They have – what do you call it – an honest marriage," as if to suggest such a thing is unusual.

I visited Rose three more times, but her later stories began conflicting with her earlier ones. She didn't say she came to the U.S. on a fiancé visa but that she came to find two of her sailor/boyfriends and "take them by surprise." She said she had a visitor's visa, not a fiancé visa. The story she told about getting to Bremerton conflicted with the story I learned from the Barios couple who befriended her on her arrival. She said Valery was born by Caesarian section, possibly confusing that delivery with her more recent one at the Navy hospital in Bremerton.

She claimed to have had an affair for years with a Seattle judge named Gary Little, whom she said she met while visiting Richard in the Kitsap jail before his extradition to Montana. "He winked at me and I winked back. I was really hooked on the judge. I was young. I wanted money, booze, drugs, nice clothes, expensive perfume. Gary gave me all of this, everything I needed—$1,000, $5,000. But he was a powerful guy, with guns and drugs. I messed up with him. I didn't know he was a bad guy."

There *was* a Judge Gary Little in King County Superior Court in Seattle, a man who shot himself in the head in 1988 in a deserted hallway of the county courthouse when he learned that a Seattle newspaper was about to publish allegations of sexual misconduct. Over the preceding six years Little had been criticized or disciplined for improper contacts with juvenile defendants, but the allegations focused on coercion to perform sex with young men, not women.

If there was substance to the allegations, as his suicide might suggest, it doesn't seem likely that he would have been amenable to an expensive affair with a woman. Besides, the attorney who handled Rose's unsuccessful appeal told me she was in and out of reality. In one of her letters to me, she instructed me enigmatically to have dinner with Bill Gates Sr., to tell him to update his will, and to have him tell her father Ferdinand Marcos to get her out of prison, but by then Marcos had been dead for 11 years.

She claims she was introduced to Gates Sr. by Sam Binnian, the Bremerton attorney who handled some of her legal affairs after Dugeno's and Erickson's deaths, that Binnian was the go-between when Gates Sr. needed to contact her and arrange for dinner together and a night at Seattle's expensive Olympic Hotel. She claims she had a four-year affair with Gates Sr., in his fifties then and married, from 1977 to 1981, that Gates Sr. is the biological father of Valery and of the infant who died of SIDS in 1983 while Rose was in a jail cell waiting to hear her sentence.

Richard Manthie did acknowledge in a letter to me that Valery was not his biological child, that when she was born in May 1978, he adopted her as his own. It's possible he was collaborating somehow with Rose on this point to lay groundwork for a future claim on Gates's estate with Valery as the beneficiary.

163

Assuming a normal gestation, the infant who died when Rose was convicted would have been conceived in April 1982. By that time, Edmondson had been dead for more than three months and Manthie had been arrested and jailed by then, so allowing for some fuzziness in Rose's memory of the dates of her supposed affair with Gates Sr., the timeline could add a little credibility to the alleged illicit relationship. With nothing more to go on, we can only speculate, keeping in mind her version of a privileged childhood as the daughter of a famous and powerful man, her attempts to wheedle money out of men by charging them with paternity of her daughters, her fantastical illusions of links to powerful men and her desire to see Valery in the will of a wealthy man, all reflecting the wide gap between her real world and her dream world. It seems likely she has dreams that by morning become reality.

So after my third visit with Rose, I decided I couldn't rely on her for the truth about herself or about her case and that her stories would be useful only for what they revealed about her state of mind, a state of mind adorned in fantasy.

She liked the idea of a book being written about her, even without knowing whether the portrayal would be positive or negative but apparently thinking it couldn't be anything but positive. She wrote several times to the Montel Williams television show, eager for the attention her appearance would provide. ("I'm good luck to colored people," she said. "They're attracted to me.") She saw her story being told in a movie and named two women who she thought could portray her, one of them an attractive, brown-skinned television news broadcaster in Seattle, the other a famous actress in the Philippines. This fact caused one psychiatrist to classify Rose as a histrionic personality, a person who sees herself as the leading character in a drama.

She told me of a car trip through Oregon once with Manthie, when the engine caught fire and a local television station was there to film the event. As Rose told the story, she was excited about the prospect of appearing on television, even in a news story. As she said, "My life is a soap opera."

My third conversation with her took place in a small room off the large visitors room where we had a view of a courtyard and other buildings – the library, the cafeteria, the gym, and the pod where Rose lived. As we talked, she was easily distracted by others who passed outside: a male guard ("I hate him.) and other inmates ("That one got 15 years for pulling a gun in a fight with her husband. He was a sheriff.")

In tracing her route from the Philippines to Bremerton, she leapt right over her marriage to Pete Dugeno and her association with Erickson, as if neither ever existed, but talked about Richard Manthie, what a handsome, sexually exciting man he was, and how she encouraged him to be a model, another prospect she found glamorous.

As she did with other visitors and those she wrote to, she expected a favor. She wanted me to take her typewriter to a repair shop but didn't have money to pay for repairs because she'd lost some of her income while in the hole for 10 days. She asked for $10 in quarters for snacks from the vending machines. She wanted me to visit all four homes where she'd lived in Kitsap County, to take photos of them and bring her the pictures.

Finally, she inquired about my children (I'd never mentioned having children) and with a conspiritorial smile, she asked if my wife were jealous over these meetings of ours.

Whether Rose's distortions of reality were conscious or not, and whether they reveal her as incorrigible and an ongoing danger to society, we have another source of information that I assume is reliable: Her prison disciplinary file. It contains reports on her behavior at regular intervals, usually about five months. After seventeen years in prison, Rose's file was about a foot thick, four times thicker than other inmates' for the same period. In her case, it portrays a person utterly immune to the restorative efforts of a correctional facility.

In one review period, she was caught with a large paper bag containing 14 boiled eggs, two lemons, two tomatoes, and several pieces of broccoli, all stolen from the kitchen. She was directed to a holding cell for a search but resisted several times. "Why? Why? I didn't do anything." While she was resisting handcuffs, several more items fell out of her pant legs – a sandwich, a package of meat, and a package of tortillas. A continuing search turned up a package of seven eggs in her bra. In her defense, she said she was taking the food to a friend for her birthday. Her penalty was 30 days in segregation.

On another occasion a guard spotted her leaving the kitchen with a large lump in her pants. She said she has having her period, that the lump was a pad. A search showed she was smuggling six cooked sausages and a large quantity of cooked bacon.

At one point she was fired from her job in the kitchen for theft, threatening other inmates, harassing them sexually, and possessing a weapon.

Other infractions included forgery, possessing unauthorized pills, being in an unauthorized area, possession of an unauthorized tool, lying to a staff member, ordering goods ("Playgirl" magazine and other items) with an unauthorized credit card, ordering items from the canteen without the funds to pay for them, telling lies that caused another inmate to be prosecuted, threatening to kill another inmate, and refusing a body search – although on another occasion she gave a written, un-required consent to a cavity search "by a nurse using her fingers or simple instruments (e.g. otoscope, tongue blade, short nasal speculum, or simple forceps) to detect contraband or any other foreign item."

Once she was caught leaving the gym with a $10 video concealed in her pants – "Claudia Shiffer Perfectly Fit Abs."

Contraband is a continual problem in prisons, and Rose's cell was searched often for items that weren't allowed there. Guards found state-issue T shirts, sweatshirt and sweatpants; sneakers, a pair of six-inch scissors, a pair of jeans, some "blue pills," hemorrhoidal suppositories hidden in a sock, a tube of hydrocortisone cream, a package of guitar strings, and a package of cheese and cookies.

Another search turned up a Tacoma Community College diploma that Rose had stolen from another inmate to use as barter for a blue T-shirt belonging to the other inmate. In the same search, guards found two clocks (one broken), some Christmas seals, and a bent wire coat hanger being used as a TV antenna.

Her frequent response: The items were planted in her cell. "They were after me because of personal conflicts we had in the past," she wrote in her defense. "They like easy living, dope, sex. They are opposite, evil people." It wasn't clear whether she was referring to other inmates or to guards.

Once she was accused of sexual harassment after giving a male guard a hand-made card bearing on the front the words, "I searched everywhere for the perfect gift." Inside, following her inscription, "Te amo mucho," was her drawing of part of a "nude woman with pendulous breasts and a black furry crotch," the guard wrote in his report. Beneath the drawing: "And it was right here all along. Enjoy. Love you. R.E." Her notes often carried citations of Biblical verses and little hearts

She had a vendetta with another inmate housed in the maximum-security unit. "Whore Madame Snitch," she wrote "I am going to kill this bitch whore madam snitch that is worthy to do time for real murder beef. I open her mouth and cut her tongue out and shove it to her itchy snitch cunt." Rose admitted writing the letter but claimed she was just joking, that she was speaking to herself. She said repeatedly that she was not a problem inmate, that she was not a violent person. She was judged guilty of threats of murder and mutilation.

Another report says she accused two staff members, a man and a woman, of having oral sex and claims she herself was sexually assaulted.

168

Apparently she got nowhere with the grievance counselor, a person Rose said disliked her. She accused the counselor of "cruel, sadistic and immature behavior."

Some of her periodic reports showed no infractions of prison rules and indicated efforts at improving herself. She took courses in reading, math, English, American history, consumer education, and individual education through Tacoma Community College and "...has adjusted in an acceptable manner and is performing in a satisfactory manner," one report states. But the same report says, "Not involved in any special therapy ...has not been receptive to counseling and is thus not open to therapy ... Leisure time is spent comrading [sic] with peers and watching television."

She writes letters, many letters. During her first few years in prison she regularly sent things to the head of the Kitsap County jail (where she spent most of her time in the hole for violation of rules) – homemade Christmas cards, drawings, religious pamphlets, and little items she'd made in a crafts class.

She wrote to Edmondson's former friend and roommate Mike Cogswell, sending him books and crosses, insisting on her innocence, saying that she loved him and, in a clumsy attempt to pin parenthood on him, saying that their daughters needed him.

She wrote to Edmondson's mother and stepfather ("Dear Mom and Dad"), assuring them of her love for Bill and that he sleeps with her and talks to her all the time. She told them she wasn't mad at them and reminded them that she lost a son too. She rejected responsibility for Edmondson's death and placed all the blame on Manthie, who she said killed Bill out of jealousy and hatred and the need to get revenge on Rose for her marrying Bill. He told her that no one was going to have her but him, she wrote, and that if she implicated him in the crime he would kill her and Valery and burn down their two houses. Manthie had a lot of mafia friends throughout Kitsap County, she claimed, and said she was scared to death.

To Bill Edmondson's brother James, she complained about a nervous breakdown and gynecological problems and how the stress of prison life was killing her little by little. She enclosed a power of attorney document and told him she had been born again and was now a full, truly saved Christian.

To Leonard Kruse, the judge in Manthie's trial, she wrote to request the appointment of a public defender to file a paternity suit against Keith Ryan and force him to support her two daughters in the Philippines. She accused one of her lawyers in her probate matters of stealing thousands of dollars from her, of lying to her, threatening her, and forcing her to sign documents she didn't understand. She was railroaded by the Kitsap justice system, she complained. There was bribery and money under the table, she wrote, and added, "Money talks, bullshits walks," and enigmatically, "the car won't run with no gas, the same of people."

She told Judge Kruse that she had been instructed by the White House and the Federal Bureau of Prisons to ask if there were some way he could investigate the case. Everyone lied, she said – the prosecutors, the police, the insurance people, her ex-boyfriends, Manthie's cellmates, and all the other witnesses.

He responded to each of her letters with kindness, even with apologies that he hadn't replied sooner. He suggested various routes she could take to get free legal assistance and explained he simply had no authority to grant her requests.

Rose wrote to others she believed would have the authority to see the cruel injustice of her conviction and set her free: President Reagan, Ferdinand Marcos, Washington Governors Dan Evans and Gary Locke, the head of the state's Department of Corrections, the appellate court, and lawyers who had represented her in the past. She denied her crime, said her trial lawyer was incompetent, and claimed the system was out to get her because she's a Filipino. Just as she was innocent of the charges against her in prison, she was innocent in the murder of her husband.

One recipient of frequent letters was Keith Ryan, one of her American sailor boyfriends at Olongapo, who she claims fathered her two daughters there, a claim Ryan denies, saying he was at sea when the girls would have been conceived. Some time in 1985, Rose located him and began a series of letters imploring him to support their two daughters, as evidenced by a notarized affidavit stating "I hereby authorize Keith W. Ryan to act in all matters with the concern for our children and with full power of attorney." She signed the document Rosaline Dugeno Manthie Edmondson. At the time, the two girls were 13 and 12 and still living in the

Philippines, but Rose told me that when she was 17 and two months pregnant with her second child, her first child died of asthma because Ryan wouldn't go for medical help. She still thinks of him as a murderer, she said, even though her many letters to him from prison are addressed to "Dearest Keith."

In one of Rose's many letters to him, she claims he hurt her deeply, that she isn't a greedy person, that she was in prison because of Manthie and his possessiveness of her.

 She reminds him that he is the legal father of the two girls and gives him the name and address of one of the lawyers who worked for her, saying that he will handle everything.

She tried flattery, commenting on his good looks and his blue eyes, and how, when they went bar hopping, she had to fight off other girls who wanted to sit with him, how she fought one off by throwing a beer bottle in her face and Ryan had to break them up. She referred to these as "the good times."

She quoted a few platitudes from her grandmother about not crying over spilled milk, then began an indictment of the Washington State legal system, accusing it of bribery, pay-offs, money under the table, and various kinds of corruption, then says she just keeps her spirits up with the knowledge that one day, she will be freed.

She instructed Ryan to tell his jealous wife she has no interest in him anymore, and she finished with a plea that he not forget the two girls and urged that he get them to the United States, giving him names and addresses of friends and relatives who would help. In a P.S., she added that the hell of prison had caused her stress and anxiety, and she sent

172

God's blessings to him and his family. Take it easy and don't work too hard, she said.

Her frequent, ongoing pleas for financial help for the two girls eventually exasperated Ryan' wife, who wrote the warden, asking her to prevent Rose from sending such letters. It didn't work, and Rose's letters became more impassioned, more laden with pathos. She asked Ryan to take the girls, admitting she'd been nasty in the past, even evil, and she apologized for that but added that she now had leukemia. She turned to the Bible and the injunction to love one another and your neighbors and your enemies, and she said she had changed, giving her life to Jesus Christ.

Another tactic was to ask adult friends in the Philippines to send letters to Ryan on behalf of the two girls, ages 13 and 11. These letters, addressed to "Dear Daddy," offered warmest greetings and the hope that he was in good health. They expressed confidence that Ryan would make the best daddy in the whole world, asked for money for new clothes and new shoes for school, and said how much they missed him, sending kisses to him and "Mom." Presumably "Mom" referred to Ryan's wife, a woman the girls had never met.

When the older daughter reached high school a few years later, Ryan received a plea for money to buy a school uniform, asking him for understanding about their dire financial straits and pleading for money, even a few dollars a month.

As she so often did, Rose undermined her own cause by sending Ryan photocopies of birth certificates for the two girls. Each girl has a certificate of live birth identifying Ryan as the father, but another birth certificate for the older girl lists a different man as the father. Again, Rose may not have known who the father was in either case and thought that casting a broad net was the best approach.

At one point Rose used a more aggressive strategy, writing to Ryan's wife and threatening to have the girls' blood tested to prove that Ryan was their father. She accused Ryan's wife of jealousy, greed, hypocrisy, and being a cold-blooded bitch. All you white people are the same, she wrote, then expressed pride in the Philippines and in her having worked as a prostitute to support her family. If Ryan's wife were going to be this way, Rose wrote, she would sue and also write President Reagan, Philippines President Ferdinand Marcus, and then-Washington Governor Dan Evans, reminding Ryan's wife that this was serious business.

In another letter to Ryan's wife, she claimed innocence in Edmondson's murder, blaming it on Manthie. She complained that prison officials were "messing" with her mail and that because of Mrs. Ryan's letter to the warden, Rose was "written up." She did her cause no good when she expressed relief that Ryan didn't give her syphilis or AIDS, when she claimed that because he was uncircumcised, it stank when she gave him oral sex, and when she accused him of being a lying, phony bi-sexual. She concluded with an abrupt change of tone, praying for her to have a long life, sending God's blessings, and saying, "Write me, OK?"

In her unceasing quest for money, whether for her daughters or herself, Rose wrote essentially

174

the same letter to two different couples in the Philippines, asking for a loan so she could hire a lawyer to get out of prison. If they were dying of kidney failure, she said, she would give them hers as a family friend and a member of God's kingdom. She said that when she had property and power, she shared it with them, appealing to their conscience for prayers and financial help to get out of prison and reminding them she is their sister in Christ Jesus.

When her "mother" Joyce Elton died, Elton's daughter-in-law sent me a box of letters Rose had written her. Some envelopes contained nothing but strange newspaper clippings and jewelry ads with rings, earrings and necklaces marked. Another contained nine pages of definitions copied verbatim from a law dictionary and a clipping headed "Chart of the Mysterious Kundalini and the Location of the Glands." In one letter she referred to her son, Shane Michael Aldrich, being 18 now, even though the child died of SIDS in infancy.

She needed deodorant, lotion, a rosary and a St. Christopher's medal, she said. She wanted pictures of the house on Long Lake Road and the house on This-A-Way. She needed eye glasses and false teeth, she said (the old ones were lost), and a copy of Black's Law Dictionary. President George W. Bush had signed her clemency papers, she said, but the guards were continuing to hold her because they were prejudiced against Asians and besides they were "vindictive, vicious, selfish killers" who had murdered seven of her friends. She enclosed a letter she had written to the Assistant Superintendant, saying she needed his TLC and wanted him to make love to her for 20 years, and she likened her love for him to God's love for humanity.

She regretted marrying Edmondson, she said, but she was a new person now and when they were pardoned, she and Richard would travel the world, and she would pay a lawyer three million dollars when they got out.

From a letter Rose wrote in April 2002, we can infer that Joyce Elton had had enough of collect calls and had put a block on calls from the prison.

Sometimes Rose relied on others like Joyce Elton to deliver communications to and from Richard at the Washington State prison in Monroe. A letter she wrote to Elton in 2002 claimed that Richard had terminal cancer, but there are obvious reasons for us to be skeptical. In that same month she said that Edmondson's real killer was Robert Yates, Jr., a serial killer in Spokane who killed 13 women (in the late 1990s, about 15 years after Edmondson's murder) and whom Rose could have learned about from newspapers and television.

In some letters she complained about her health – about depression, diabetes, a cyst on her ovaries, an ulcer, and colon problems, all credible complaints given the stress of prisons where inmates age much faster than people on the outside. A 60-year-old prisoner who had been incarcerated as long as she had might easily have the body of a 70-year-old. But as always with Rose, skepticism is prudent.

In one of her last letters to Elton, she complained of having spent 10 days in the hole because of bad roommates – sometimes she was in isolation for as long as 40 days – and commented on how the prison was getting worse because there were a lot of new young guards with no manners. She has claimed she was impregnated by one of the guards, and she told Joyce Elton that for a time she had been housed in the psychiatric ward for treatment of mental illness, a plausible report, given that her file showing prescriptions for antidepressant and antipsychotic drugs.

In 2000, after serving 17 years of a life sentence, Rose appealed to the governor for clemency. In her application, Rose pointed out correctly that until she was found guilty of Bill Edmondson's murder, she had never before been convicted of a crime. (The three theft charges were dropped after her murder conviction and her life sentence without parole, so she could technically argue that she was a first time offender.) Together, she and Manthie had spent about 40 years in prison, an excessive penalty, she believed, especially, as she put it, when "only one person was killed."

Her nine-page application on a standard government form gives us a view of the world according to Rose. In the space asking about prior criminal history, she wrote "none," which was technically true. Despite all her conniving, the threats of violence, the fights and the drug use, the thefts the victims never reported, the three theft charges in 1982, the only crime for which she had ever been tried and convicted was the aggravated first-degree murder of her husband.

Was a weapon used during the commission of the crime?

"Yes. 22 caliber gun."

Were you under the influence of drugs or alcohol at the time of the offense?

"Yes. I was drunk & pills."

If incarcerated, present status:

"Married"

State government records show that on October 17, 1994, she married a Roger Keith McAbee in a ceremony in the prison chapel witnessed by about ten guests, video taped, followed by dancing and, for the newlyweds, a conjugal visit in a special house trailer at the prison. One of the witnesses of the ceremony was a Filipino woman from Bremerton who visited Rose several times merely as a Christian duty, but she said she wouldn't want to be considered a friend of Rose whose conversations about sex made her uncomfortable, and she believes the relationship was never consummated.

This woman was part of a Filipino social service organization when Rose arrived in Kitsap County, and like so many others, she received some of Rose's many importunities: Please lend me money for a ring for my prison wedding. Please lend me $10,000 to fund my appeal. Please fly to Idaho to visit my daughter there. Please buy me the following items: (The value of the items on her list often exceeded $100.) Please buy the land my new husband owns here in Washington. The friend declined all these requests.

At Rose's urging, she did visit the property allegedly owned by McAbee's family, and she spent some time praying with them, but she said it looked more like five acres of land rather than the 100 acres

Rose claimed, and she said the family appeared very poor.

One report held that Rose made the mistake of giving her only copy of her trial transcript to her new husband who, according to rumors, was a retarded man who stood to inherit land in Washington's Pierce County. McAbee allegedly showed the transcript to his mother who, on learning that Rose was a murderer motivated by a desire for money and property, had the marriage annulled. Another version, relayed by Rose's daughter Valery in one of my two phone conversations before I lost touch with her, is that McAbee's 80-year-old mother owned 88 acres, not five, and that according to her neighbors, son Roger was caught operating a drug lab. Washington state records do show that he was arrested in October 2000 on a controlled substance violation.

State records show no evidence of McAbee's divorce from a previous marriage to another woman in 1981 before he married Rose in 1994, and all my efforts to locate McAbee have failed.

When I located Valery by phone, she was singularly articulate, gracious and helpful, a loyal daughter who had been studying psychology and seemed fully aware of her mother's deeds and shortcomings. She added that her father's version of events would be very different from her mother's. She urged me to contact the McAbees in the Carolinas, saying they would be rich sources of information, but it seemed there were hundreds of McAbees there, and when I called her again, the man who answered said she'd left and he didn't know where she'd gone.

Do you have employment if your petition is granted? the clemency petition form asked.

"Yes. Harrison Hospital in Bremerton."

Her response would have provided great amusement at the hospital.

Attempting to demonstrate her rehabilitation, she cited her participation in Inside/Out Industries and the K-9 dog program, and her work in the prison kitchen and the prison library and as a prison groundskeeper and prison custodian. She says she graduated from a "moral recognition therapy program" and a chemical dependency program, that she regularly attended meetings of Alcohol Anonymous and Narcotics Anonymous, that she went to monthly prayer meetings and Bible study sessions, and that each month she talked with her sponsors and the Native American Indian Sisterhood.

Even though she had abandoned her two daughters when she left them behind in Philippines in 1977, she also listed the older one, now a resident of the U.S., as a reference and claimed that had been invited to live with her and her husband whenever she wanted after her release, a claim that flatly contradicted what the daughter told me by phone in a stunningly brief conversation: She wanted nothing to do with her mother. Rose said that the other daughter, still in the Philippines, died of an asthma attack when her husband failed to get her emergency medical treatment.

Another reference listed was Joyce Elton, the woman who was so generous and kind to Rose in the past and who traveled across the country with her to attend Edmondson's funeral in Pennsylvania, and to whom Rose had sent so many letters and birthday cards from prison. But by this time, Elton had made herself unavailable to Rose, having tired of Rose's incessant importunities: "Bring me this, buy me that, come and visit me, call my lawyer and tell him to get me out of this hell hole."

The final part of her clemency petition was a letter addressed to President Bill Clinton and Governor Gary Locke in which she thought her sentence without the chance for parole was exceptional for a first time offender and that she had been subjected to "Cruel Inhumane Maltreatment punishment" in prison and was the object of "Riverse Discrimination by the prosecutor."

In this letter she accused her trial lawyer of failing to investigate the case and to discover "a substantial number of witnesses," of making a "calculated decision not to present a more substantial mitigation" defense, and of overlooking her good character traits and specific examples of her compassion. And, she said, the crime hadn't been properly charged, that it was *not* aggravated first-degree murder, and that it "was not particularly cruel or heinous."

She concludes, "As you can see, I have done many things to prepare myself for re-entry into society and that I have a loving family waiting for me to come home. I believe I have done my time and that I can be a productive member of society with the skills I have learned in prison. I am asking you to consider me for the clemency pardon & parole program. I pray to Father GOD."

By this point, you know much more about Rose and Manthie than the jurors heard at trial, and given her prison disciplinary file, you would undoubtedly deny her clemency. But suspend what you know, if you can, and for the moment forget about the Washington state statute pertaining to first-degree murder and the broad range of sentences in this country for murder in the first degree, from a minimum of 20 years to the death penalty.

Because Richard Manthie has denied my requests to visit him, and because we have no access to information about his adjustment to prison life, I know only what one of his visitors said – that he has used his time to learn jewelry making and is trying to find markets for his work on the outside. Joyce Elton's daughter took some of his jewelry to farmers' markets for sale but had little luck.

As for Rose, while I have a lot of reliable information about her after she arrived in this country, I have much less about her earlier life in the Philippines, and some of that is unreliable. If we could fill in those gaps, we would have a much better understanding of these two murderers, and maybe of how they came to be where they are.

* * *

Rose's clemency hearing was held in the Cherberg Senate Office Building next to the golden-domed state capitol building at Olympia in the summer of 2001. In a long, narrow room, 15 rows of chairs faced one end where the Governor's Clemency and Pardon Board of six men and two women sat behind a table on a raised platform, a wood paneled wall behind them. The Board hears numerous appeals on the same day. Observers sign in and identify the name of the petitioner whose case they

182

have come to support or merely to hear. Not one of Rose's former friends or acquaintances was there to hear the outcome.

All eight board members had read the files on all the petitioners, the Chairman explained, and the meeting was now open to visitors who wanted to speak in favor of or against any petitioner. When Rose's application came up, the first to speak was Christian Casad, one of the two county attorneys who had prosecuted her case 17 years earlier. Casad was a little over six feet, bald now, with brown hair around the edges, glasses, and rings on both ring fingers. During the years since the trial, he had grown bigger around the waist than at the shoulders.

Casad pointed out that Rose's crime was planned, cold, calculated, brutal, and motivated by her lust for profit, and that life without parole was an appropriate sentence. When he began summarizing her story, explaining how she visited Manthie in prison on the first night of her honeymoon with the victim, the Chairman cut him off, reminding him that all the Board members had read the file.

The only other one to speak was Kitsap County Sheriff Steve Boyer, dressed in his brown uniform to represent law enforcement. Boyer is tall with a sharp nose, dark hair neatly trimmed, and a ready smile. Normally an open, loquacious man who loves campaigning and doesn't spare words, on this day, in responding to Rose's petition, he was uncharacteristically brief. His entire testimony, verbatim and unabridged: "My name is Steve Boyer. I'm the sheriff of Kitsap County. My job is to keep the peace. If this woman is released, my job will be much harder."

There were no questions from the Board. One member noted Rose's numerous infractions in prison and her threats to other inmates, all in conflict with Rose's self-portrait as somebody who gets along with everyone. The Board's decision to deny her petition was unanimous. Rose's case took a mere six minutes.

Obviously, in Rose's case, the Clemency Board, having read her prison file, saw no improvement in her behavior, no social adjustment that would make her a safe bet for release. In her mind, as we saw in her petition for clemency, there is a cavernous gap between how she sees herself and how prison officials see her. In her mind, all her troubles are attributable to someone else: Richard Manthie, a corrupt legal system, an inept trial attorney, rampant discrimination against Filipinos, a cruel, racist, and an unfair prison staff that has it in for her.

In these contrasting perceptions of a murderer on one hand and the judicial/penal system on the other, we're quick to side with the latter; but could there be some truth on the murderer's side? Was the Clemency Board given a fair and balanced picture? Might the prison staff be as cruel and vindictive as she depicted them? Might her experience in prison have changed her enough to enable her to adapt to society without being a danger, to fit in harmlessly and productively?

Two years later, Rose wrote again to Leonard Kruse, the judge in Manthie's trial, not hers, apparently because his kind responses to her earlier had given her hope. She asked him to amend the judgment against her, explaining that she was now a Christian woman, that she had been diagnosed with diabetes, and that she was missing out on her children's lives. Besides, she said, when she claimed innocence in Edmondson's death, she didn't understand that if convicted she might get a life sentence without the possibility of parole. She was "mental and unstable" at the time and didn't understand that she could have agreed to a lesser charge and get just 10 years. "When I learned that, I was devastated," she said.

In 2009 she sought relief again, asking that her penalty be reduced because of "current life circumstances," because her solicitation of Manthie to murder Edmondson was not an aggravating factor, and because she had ineffective counsel.

Her most recent petition, filed in 2010, claimed she had new evidence. She wanted her conviction reversed and the charge against her dismissed, saying the laws under which she was convicted were unconstitutional. All these petitions have been unsuccessful. But as long as she has the time, access to the prison library, and the energy to try again, she's free to carry on this futile struggle from her self-created hell.

NINE

Washington Corrections Center for Women, 2013

Thirteen years after my first visit with Rose, I visited her again, curious to see what 30 years of prison life had done to her, but mainly to dig deeper for details to stories she'd told me earlier.

Dressed in a gray, prison-issue sweat suit, she greeted me with a big smile and a hug as she did before, then led me to the table assigned to us, number 24. There were about 40 tables in the visiting room now, smaller ones for two people, larger ones for four or six, all arranged in neat rows. As before, the first order of business was to go to the vending machines for sandwiches, candy and soft drinks.

Surprisingly, Rose looked better than she did 13 years earlier. Her skin was clear and healthy looking, her hands were well manicured, her hair dyed black with a little gray still showing at the roots. While other inmates wore prison-issued white T-shirts and gray sweat pants, Rose wore a tan, loose-fitting jacket that concealed her plumpness. She bought a hot dog from the vending machine, heated it in the microwave, added a bottle of Squirt and a candy bar, and we returned to table 24 to talk. She was more at ease than in my three visits years earlier, with herself and with me, calmer, more naturally friendly, not trying so hard to be cute and beguiling.

Over the years she had seen many women come and go, some for just a year, others for maybe three

186

or four. Of the 854 inmates, 150 had been convicted of either first or second Degree murder. By this time, only 23 of the 858 inmates are older than Rose, who was 58, and none has been there as long.

No, she said, she hadn't had any visitors, and she hadn't heard from Valery for years, although her older daughter, one who was born in the Philippines and who now lives in this country, sent her s she will come for a visit. She hasn't seen Roger McAbee either. Her version was that he had the marriage annulled when the state abolished conjugal visits after an inmate in another state prison strangled his wife during a conjugal visit after she told him she was divorcing him.

She has no means of communicating with Richard and that's fine with her, she said with both finality and resentment. If it weren't for him, she said, she wouldn't be in prison now. "Didn't you help him kill Bill?" I asked. No, she said. "He just told me to clean up the mess." I think she now believes that to be true, that she has pushed aside her part in all the scheming that led to the murder.

Yet she had a surprising memory of other things – dates of certain events, for example, and details of the relationship she claims to have had with Bill Gates, Sr. She was introduced to him by Sam Binnian, she said, the Seattle attorney who handled some of her legal affairs before her trial for murder, and by John Henry Browne.

She remembers when the affair began, and because Manthie was never around, how easy it was to slip away for meetings with Gates at the elegant Olympic Hotel in Seattle. In her mind, it's clear that Gates Sr. is the father of the short-lived Shane

Michael Edmondson, born while she was in the Kitsap jail waiting for the verdict in her murder trial.

Rose's assertion that Gates was Valery's father rang a faint bell in my memory of a letter I received from Manthie after asking for an interview. After searching my files, I found his letter of 2002 in which he wrote, "I will discuss with you anything involving this case and my marriage with Rose and that includes the adoption of my daughter Valery Manthie." (He changed his mind and the interview never took place.) So Manthie knew that someone else had fathered this child who now was his, but given Rose's promiscuity it could have been one of many men. Rose finds hope in believing it was a man of wealth and influence who, if he knew about Valery, would do the right thing and leave his wealth to her. This imaginary legacy is all she has to leave to her daughter.

In 2013, after locating Valery again, I wrote to her, but she didn't respond so I know only this about her: She has taken the surname of the family that raised her; she is a beautiful, statuesque woman of 34 who has won a state beauty pageant; and she teaches elementary age children in a private school.

As of now, I appear to be Rose's only contact with the outside world, and she accords me influence I simply don't have: The authority to knock on the door of Bill Gates, Sr., tell him about Valery, and expect him to shower her with money. Even if he were the father, Rose never considered the idea that he would simply deny it and call for security.

She reached her hands across the table to hold mine. "You will be a rich man," she insisted several times with great conviction, envisioning not just a book but also a movie from which she and I would share the proceeds. I explained that Washington law prohibited a convicted criminal from profiting by the sale of her story. The news seemed to deflate her.

But there may have been other reasons for her sullenness in my last meeting with her. I explained to her again that it wasn't my intent to aid in her early release from prison, that my job was merely to tell her story, and that her story wasn't a flattering one. I think she was finally facing reality, that her efforts to use me as an agent on her behalf weren't working. She hugged me again when I left, but it was a cooler hug, and a few days later she wrote to say she would no longer cooperate with me on this book but that she hoped we could still be friends.

EPILOGUE

Assessing Rose

Mental health experts will quickly recognize Rose as a distinctive personality type, even though they might disagree on which slot to put her in. Some would describe her as having antisocial personality disorder. Some would almost certainly label her a psychopath, others a sociopath, while still others use those two terms interchangeably. Those who see her as psychopathic—there is abundant supporting evidence in her story—estimate that there are about 2,000,000 of them in North America, 100,000 in New York City alone.

Hearing "psychopath," many think of Jeffrey Dahmer, the convicted cannibal and necrophiliac; John Wayne Gacy Jr., the rapist who murdered 33 boys and men, 29 of whom were found buried in the crawl space of his house; or Ted Bundy, the serial killer and rapist who confessed to 30 murders but may have murdered many more and may have mutilated and molested the bodies after their deaths

Noah Rubenstein, a licensed marriage and family therapist, estimates that one out of 100 men and one out of 300 women are psychopaths. Dr. Martha Stout, a clinical psychologist at Harvard and the author of "The Sociopath Next Door," says the incidence is even higher, one out of 25. But they're hardly all Jeffrey Dahmers, John Wayne Gacys or Ted Bundys. The disorder appears in all races, all populations, all income levels, and the chances are that each of us has met at least one in our lives. They

190

may be teachers, soldiers, physicians, business executives, lawyers, blue-collar workers, or religious leaders, but they all share most of the symptoms characteristic of psychopaths: They're glib, superficial, egocentric, grandiose, and lacking an ability to feel empathy, remorse or guilt. They're deceitful, manipulative and impulsive, with a need for excitement. They have minimal ability to control their behavior, and they lack the ability to feel responsibility for their actions. Rather than feel guilt or regret for taking advantage of others, they scorn their victims for their gullibility. But most psychopaths aren't rapists and murderers.

Contrary to myth, they're no more intelligent than the average person, just more cunning and, with their glibness, better at manipulating others. Early in their lives, they learn that charm is an effective tool in taking advantage of other people, and that if lying or breaking the law is required to satisfy their desires, they'll lie or break the law as easily as blink. Because their emotions are shallow, they're generally not passionate in pursuing their self-indulgence, just determined. It goes without saying that psychopaths, incapable of loyalty to anyone but themselves, make poor employees, and because of their incapacity to love anyone but themselves, that they make poor spouses and parents.

All Rose's crimes, whether she was charged with them or not, were part of an aggressive campaign to satisfy her needs for money and property, a campaign in which her primary commodity of exchange was the opportunity for sex. Whether stealing money off the bar in an enlisted man's club, raiding her victim's pants pockets after a one-night stand, marrying the 76-year-old property-owner Pete Dugeno to inherit his money and property, befriending lonely and ailing property-owner Robert Erickson and worming her way into his affections and his will, or tricking the vulnerable, naïve Bill Edmondson into marriage by feigning pregnancy and love, the tactic and the goal were always the same: Using her body and guile to advance herself at others' expense. In researching her story, I found not one example of generosity or magnanimity, no moment when she put others before self. To do so would be incompatible with she is. It would be impossible.

  She used everyone who was willing to meet her needs: Her "mother" Joyce Elton, who befriended her, who loaned her money, who traveled with her across the country to attend Edmondson's funeral, who accepted collect calls from prison and visited her there many times; her fellow employees at the hospital who loaned her money; the neighbors who, after Dugeno's death, took her in and helped care for daughter Valery; her neighbors the Davis's on Long Lake Road who, for several years, were more Valery's parents than Rose was. She is a persistent taker, rarely a giver, and on the few occasions when she gave to others, it was mainly to advance her cause of taking.

  Rose unwittingly began revealing her symptoms to me on my first prison visit when she flirtatiously took me by the arm to pose for photos and, when the Polaroid images eased out of the camera, when she drew hearts and smiley faces in the margins. It was easy to imagine how lonely, randy young sailors might have responded to such an inviting approach in her youth.

When she signed a document giving me access to all her prison records, including her disciplinary file, with no curiosity how this profile might depict her, she showed no caution, no reservations. As the central figure in a book, she would be the star of her own show, and it seemed to make no difference how she'd be portrayed, as if she believed the only possible portrayal would be positive.

In one of our first meetings, she did ask if it could hurt her to cooperate with me in telling her story. I reminded her that she'd been sentenced to life without parole, so, no, this couldn't hurt her. What was important to her was the idea of becoming the central figure in a story played by the Filipino actress or the Seattle news broadcaster.

In that same first meeting, when telling me that her mother died giving birth to her and saying, "God must really have loved me," she exuded a grandiosity most of us wouldn't claim, the belief that she was a favored child, chosen by God to live while her mother obviously was not.

A psychopath can be identified only by qualified clinicians, but they have some guidelines to go by. First is the kind of profile I've drawn in the preceding chapters, a profile based on Rose's lifetime of behaviors. The second is a model created by Robert D. Hare, author of "Without Conscience" and one of the leading authorities on this symptom, a model based on his work with prisoners. Hare lists these characteristic behaviors: Superficial charm

(Rose's quick, physical contact with men); a grandiose sense of self-worth ("God must really love me." "Blacks like me. I'm good luck to them."); pathological lying (the claims of her connection to Marcos); cunning, manipulative behavior (her thefts of money from men); lack of remorse or guilt (her indifference to Dugeno's, Erickson's and Edmondson's deaths); shallow, self-centered, short-lived emotions; callousness; and the inability to accept responsibility for her actions (her denial of the numerous thefts and her continued denial of any responsibility for Edmondson's death).

Hare also lists these indicators: Early behavior problems (her flight from the convent school); a parasitic lifestyle (her relationships with Pete Dugeno and Robert Erickson); a need for stimulation, poor behavioral control, impulsiveness and irresponsibility (her nightlife in bars while leaving her daughter with others); the lack of realistic long-term goals ("Tell Bill Gates Sr. to update his will." "We're going to be rich."); and criminal versatility (thefts, a life insurance scam, and murder).

Rose displays all these behaviors. But whether she's a psychopath, a sociopath, or an anti-social personality makes no difference to the law as long as it's determined she knew right from wrong at the time of her crimes. Her ability to distinguish wrong from right is shown by her efforts to conceal or deny her crimes; she just doesn't *care* about such distinctions when they're inconvenient, when they get in the way of reaching her goals. Neither she nor her lawyer ever make a claim of an impaired mental state, never claimed that alcohol and drugs erased or mitigated her responsibility for Edmondson's death.

Most experts in psychopathy agree on these two significant points: Psychopaths do not choose their disorder, and they are immune to treatment, especially by the time they have reached adulthood. It's the conscience that helps keep us moral and on the right side of the law, that allows us to empathize and to do good for others and put them above ourselves without expecting payback. Anyone who has been deprived of a conscience and is fated to stay that way deserves some sympathy, whatever her crimes.

While mental health experts mostly agree on the characteristics of psychopathy, they disagree on the *cause*. Some argue that the disorder results from social or environmental forces in very early childhood. Others find the cause in biology, pointing out that EEG's show that in people diagnosed as psychopaths, brain structures have matured at a slower rate, possibly as a result of injury to the front of the brain. (Remember that Richard Manthie suffered minor brain injury at age two.) Lesions in the orbitofrontal part of the brain's prefrontal cortex impair the inhibition of socially unacceptable behavior. In addition, parts of the brain – the prefrontal cortex and the amygdala – are small in people considered psychopaths. But whatever differences mental health experts have about causes, they agree that whatever the disorder is called, it is a syndrome, a cluster of related symptoms.

M. Craig and others reported in "Modern Psychiatry" that psychological and neuro-imaging experiments reveal in psychopaths a diminished responsiveness to fearsome or other negative stimuli. They might react to an emotional word like "rape" just as they would to a neutral word like "chair," and when faced with an impending electrical shock, they don't register heightened skin conduction due to sweating as others would. These writers consider psychopathy an innate condition that precludes empathy, conscience, and the control of impulse.

But Hare has found no convincing evidence that social or environmental factors alone produce psychopathy. Instead, he says, "… it results from a complex but poorly understood interplay between biological and social factors," that they "both play a role in what nature has provided."

They do agree on this: That adult psychopaths are incorrigible, that their condition is irremediable. If imprisoned, they may appear to be amenable to therapy, either individually or in groups, but therapy sessions are merely opportunities to polish their skills at duping others, including the therapists who can be instrumental in declaring them recovered and recommending their early release. Some are good at it and succeed. Rose is not.

The Kitsap County Sheriff knew that when he explained at Rose's clemency hearing that his job of keeping the peace would be much harder if she were at large again. The clemency board obviously agreed.

But then we have this question: If Rose is diagnosed a psychopath and if treatment is futile, if she is destined by lack of conscience to continue the kind of behavior that sent her to prison, if a defective brain structure or some other irreversible factor is responsible for her condition, is it just to punish her for behaviors she can't moderate or control? I'll return to that question in a moment.

Like Rose, Richard Manthie showed numerous signs of the psychopath, starting in childhood and continuing through his murder of Bill Edmondson and his denial of culpability for his earlier offenses, with this exception: According to recent visitors, he no longer blames others for his troubles, although it would be understandable if he still blamed Rose for using him as her agent in Edmondson's death.

Rose seems stable and rational sometimes, at other times confused, drifting in and out of reality, maybe even preferring fantasy to the relentlessly harsh prison life to which she herself contributes. She has no visitors, and she hasn't heard from Valery for years. At Rose's request, I wrote Valerie again to say her mother wants to hear from her and that she has important news about her (Valery's) father (Gates Sr.). To my knowledge, there has been no response, so Rose doesn't know that despite Valery's unusual childhood, she has become a successful woman. Twenty-nine when imprisoned, almost 60 now, Rose has been a cooperative inmate at times, at other times rebellious, defiant, incorrigible, still hoping for help from her lawyer, her judge, the governor and the president, accusing the legal system of corruption, sometimes falsely believing that her case has advanced to the U.S. Supreme Court, unable to accept or understand that she will be where she is for as long as she breathes

* * *

In one sense, all murders are alike; there are, after all, no new motives under the sun, nothing new about jealousy, hate, rage, lust, greed or an uncontrollable need for revenge. Still, each murder illustrates those ancient motives in its own singular way. But *murderers* are not all alike. What is striking about this case is the profoundness of the murderer's greed, the audacity with which she pursued her ends, the ruthlessness with which she manipulated the lives of others, her immunity to the most basic values of human society, her monomania in reaching her goals, and, even in prison, her cunning but clumsy attempts to satisfy her needs at the expense of others.

I have two regrets in telling this story. The first is that I don't have more information about Richard Manthie in his post-conviction life. An interview might have told me the history of his relationship with Rose and whether he believed he loved her (if he is capable of love) or merely found her useful for sex. If the latter is the case, they were parasites feeding off one another to satisfy their own selfish needs. An interview might have told me how he feels about Rose today, and if he, like Rose, is still angry about the judicial system or if, after more than three decades, he has become resigned to his life-long imprisonment and chosen to make the best of it.

But I have a much greater regret that I can't offer a more complete picture of Bill Edmondson, the hapless victim of Rose's greed and indifference to human life and Richard Manthie's savagery. We might hope that four years in the Navy would have made him a better judge of people and immunize him against predators like Rose. But despite his shortcomings, despite his naïveté, his lack of caution, his excessive drinking, his boasting and his prevailing vulnerability, he isn't terribly different from many other young men his age. Like many of them, he was thoughtful to his mother, calling her at regular, expected times, and he was caring of Rose's daughter Valery, much more so than Rose was. He was just never given much of a shot at life. Even Rose and Richard Manthie don't deserve what they did to him. But given the nature of the two killers, if their victim hadn't been Bill Edmondson, it would have been someone very much like him, someone who found himself in their path and was susceptible to their tactics and design.

Not every psychopath is a murderer, of course. Some are successful executives, politicians, accountants, lawyers, teachers, physicians, nurses and ministers, people who commit financial crimes or just make life miserable for those around them – their spouses, children, parents, employees, patients, clients, and other prospective victims. But prison has a purpose other than punishment; even though we know many criminals will continue their patterns of antisocial behavior in prison and again if freed, we can at least enjoy protection from them for the length of their confinement. Given her inherent immunity to rehabilitation, I expect that no one would want her released and living next door.

End

Acknowledgments

Scores of people have generously provided information about the lives of Rosalina Edmondson and Richard Manthie and helped me tell this story, and I'm grateful to them all. Their names are listed in alphabetical order:

In Kitsap County

Marietta Barios, Elsie Bautista, Larry Bertholf, Ron Bright, Chris Casad, Mike Cogswell, Dave Cook, Pat Denchel, Janine Dinio, Rosalina Edmondson, Joyce Elton, Karen Elton, Jim Harris, Patty Johnson, Bonnie Lee, Dina Lopez, Leonard Kruse, Ray Magerstaedt, Joanne Marez, Wes Niquette, Andy Oakley, Roy Rainey, June Ralph, Thelma Ramos, Greg Sandstrom, Leon Smith, Alice Tiffany, and Ted Zink

News stories from The Bremerton Sun, now The Kitsap Sun, gave me the basic outline of the investigation and the two trials. The cover photo is from the Kitsap Sun.

In Montana

Allan Brockaway, Billye Ann Bricker, Milton Datsopoulas, Loryl Johnson, Helen Johnson, Louise Miles, and Patrick Miles

In Pennsylvania

Cherrie Bentler, Gary Edmondson, Cesare Forconi, Gordon Stoffet, Mark Johnson, Ken Reynolds

Others

Mark Johnson, Keith Ryan, and John Strait

In addition, these people improved the manuscript significantly by their editorial talents, saving me from uncountable embarrassments: **Sarah Nell Davis**, my brother **Don Woutat**, **Dee Coppola**, **Tina Bright**, and my unflaggingly supportive wife **Marilee Hansen**, always my first editor, who read numerous drafts of the manuscript and seemed never to tire of my innumerable retellings of the Rosalina story to others. I hope every writer has people like these behind him. Any remaining errors and shortcomings are, alas, my own.

Cover photo by The Kitsap Sun

Cover Design by Ed Morgan

Made in the USA
San Bernardino, CA
16 December 2014